MW00654578

Your success is

Inevitable!

—Jody

Inevitable

Managing the Inevitable Bumps of Life

by Jody M. Dawson

DORRANCE
PUBLISHING CO
EST. 1920
PITTSBURGH, PENNSYLVANIA 15238

The contents of this work, including, but not limited to, the accuracy of events, people, and places depicted; opinions expressed; permission to use previously published materials included; and any advice given or actions advocated are solely the responsibility of the author, who assumes all liability for said work and indemnifies the publisher against any claims stemming from publication of the work.

All Rights Reserved
Copyright © 2019 by Jody M. Dawson

No part of this book may be reproduced or transmitted, downloaded, distributed, reverse engineered, or stored in or introduced into any information storage and retrieval system, in any form or by any means, including photocopying and recording, whether electronic or mechanical, now known or hereinafter invented without permission in writing from the publisher.

Dorrance Publishing Co
585 Alpha Drive
Pittsburgh, PA 15238
Visit our website at *www.dorrancebookstore.com*

ISBN: 978-1-6453-0228-5
eISBN: 978-1-6453-0854-6

Table of Contents

Introduction

Anyone who has been roaming the earth for any period of time will tell you that life has its ups and downs. We know one of life's truths is that there will be good times and bad times. This idea has been captured in countless books, movies, stories, fairy tales, nursery rhymes, and probably over a million country music songs. Who could forget the story of *Alice in Wonderland* where the loveable Alice is sitting on the riverbank with her sister, minding her own business, when she suddenly sees a talking white rabbit bound down a hole? Upon following the white rabbit, her world is turned upside down as she enters Wonderland, where she encounters her *nemesis*, the Queen of Hearts. Or what about *The Godfather*? Michael Corleone had returned home from World War II and survived many hardships during his tenure serving our country. He reconnected with his girlfriend and was looking to live a decent, normal life away from the family business of organized crime. After repeatedly rejecting his father's requests to join the family business, he was thrust into the limelight after an attempt on his father's life and his brother's murder and forced to *perform* at the highest level of organized crime. Even still there was Humpty

Dumpty. Humpty was sitting on that wall, enjoying the view of the English countryside, when he tipped over and busted his head. Despite the best emergency medical services available at the time (the King's horses and King's men), he just wasn't able to overcome that *crisis* in his life. So whether you are a mob boss, nursery rhyme character, or just a common everyday person, there will be ups and downs in your leadership journey.

This book speaks to the business person, the parent, coach, employer, or really anyone who is in a position of leadership that will encounter hardships along the way. These "bumps" are an inevitable part of this journey that happen, whether you want them to or not.

These bumps we encounter in life are often viewed as negative and stressful and something that should be avoided if at all possible. A bump may be a layoff from your job, dealing with a difficult employee, or even a health issue impacting a loved one. People try to stay away from stress and discomfort in their lives. When confronted with any hardship or challenge, we take the path of least resistance, which is frequently the wrong path. Believe me, no one should pass judgment on anyone when it comes to facing a hardship or taking the easy route. We ALL do it. How people deal with challenges depends on an individual's past experiences, upbringing, social status, etc.

I hope people will read this book and take key points from it that they can apply to their own lives. But even more than that, I want people who read this book to think differently about these

...your happiness and outlook on life should be defined by HOW you deal with these bumps, not whether they exist.

bumps in the road. Your success or happiness in life should not be based on whether or not you have a bump in the road, because bumps are inevitable and often times beyond your control. Instead, your happiness and outlook on life should be defined by HOW you deal with these bumps, not whether they exist. The "How" matters…

So what makes me qualified to even talk about some of this stuff? I am a middle-aged dude over 40 (barely), have been a professional for over 18 years, have a wife and kids, and lead a fairly suburban lifestyle. I have encountered many challenges in my life but probably no more than the common, average person. But I have undergone a change in my life recently that I feel makes me qualified to opine on this topic. In the past, when I encountered a challenge in my life, I viewed it as very negative. Anything that didn't go *right*, was bad. In the past, my overall sense of happiness was tied directly to "how things were going" at that moment in time. If my work and home life were going well, the sun never seemed to shine so bright. My outlook on everything was positive and optimistic. Conversely, if I was going through a tough time, the skies always seemed grey and I would outwardly show the stress and annoyance of my current situation. I wear my emotions on my sleeve, and while I always try to be upbeat, these "tough" times would really bum me out. Even though I was happy outwardly, the bottom line is that inside I had negative feelings and would act really stressed out.

I even got to the point where I took anti-depressants, saw a therapist, and even turned to alcohol to cope with these peaks and valleys in my life. To say the least, I was distracted and not nearly as productive at work or as engaged at home as I should be, and the things I cared about most were suffering. I would get so frustrated, riding this roller coaster of highs and lows, especially when I seemingly had no control over any of it. I felt helpless. Then finally one day, something changed.

I was going through a tough time at work with lots of deadlines, and my home life with young kids was equally as stressful. I felt overwhelmed all the time; there was too much to do in a single day. It felt like my world was crashing down. I became depressed. But then something happened: I'm not really sure if it was because I hit rock bottom or if there was divine intervention from above or words of wisdom I received from my mentor, but I just decided I was not going to live my life this way. This pressure and stress were not unique to me, and I was smart enough and tough enough to overcome it and not let it beat me. It took me years (decades) of being frustrated and stubborn, but I finally figured enough was enough, and I found this small little thing that changed everything for me.

I love to run. I'm not the most accomplished runner in the world but have ran numerous half marathons, 10k's and 5k's, and on several occasions, run a full marathon (3:14 personal best). When talking about my races (whether it be the training or the race itself), most people would look at me like a crazy person and comment how they could never imagine running ten miles, much less 26.2 miles. Repeatedly I found myself defending my hobby and explaining why I would put myself through months of training only to endure a very painful three hours on race day. After defending my hobby for many years, it finally dawned on me that I really just liked the training more than anything. It wasn't crossing the finish line on race day that meant the most to me, although that is nice, it was the challenge of

> After years of frustration in riding the emotional roller coaster that is life, it dawned on me that this is my only ride and that I better enjoy all of it... even the *bad*.

training every day and the reward that came along with working towards a goal, being prepared, and overcoming the *obstacles* that came at me (injury, not enough training time, hills, bad weather, etc.). As it turned out, I really liked the journey of getting to the starting line more than I did crossing the finish line itself.

After years of frustration in riding the emotional roller coaster that is life, it dawned on me that this is my only ride and that I better enjoy all of it… even the *bad*. I am not alone in this thinking, but in my opinion, life should be more focused on the journey (cliché) and *enjoying* the obstacles rather than on reaching the final destination (whatever that might be for you). Think about it. When you get to the end… it's over! Why would you want to focus or be emotionally invested in the end? Shouldn't you invest in the journey? Reaching the mountaintop should not be the true goal; it is the successful and enriching climb, filled with all the bumps and struggles, that is the *real* goal. A change in mindset of embracing those challenges in life changes everything. It was this small nuance that allowed me to turn the corner and not get eaten up inside by every little challenge that came my way.

I ask you now to think about the last challenge you had in your life. Was it a crisis? Was it related to your nemesis? Maybe you had a big performance recently. Whatever the bump might be, think about it for a minute. Who was involved? What do you remember about it?

When I think back on some difficulties I've had, I view them as less significant in importance now that they've passed than I did when I was going through them. Ironically, when I get together with old friends, former co-workers, or family members, we tend to talk and laugh the most about the hard times. No one really remembers the good times, and because we've all had tough times before, they're more interesting to talk about and they typically define us as people. Whether it be the emotion, adrenaline, or memories involved, those bumps are seared into our minds and shape the major memories and the fiber of who we are.

I believe there are seven major types of challenges that all leaders will encounter. I try to dissect those issues and give some insight into what they are and how to overcome them. But if you don't have the right attitude and mindset, these challenges will eat you alive and overwhelm you. I have been there before and can promise you they will. So very simply, if you view these challenges as an opportunity and a blessing, you have a fighting chance! One of my all-time favorite stories about managing these bumps is that of Helen Keller.

Helen Keller was born on June 27th in 1880. Helen was born healthy in 1880 to a loving family in Tuscumbia, Alabama. It wasn't until she was approximately 18-months-old that she contracted an illness (it's guessed to be either scarlet fever or meningitis), which rendered her both deaf and blind. Being blind and deaf at a very young age at that time was extraordinarily difficult. Helen was lucky to grow up in a loving home where her parents did not view her disabilities as shortcomings, and they made significant efforts to help her navigate the daily challenges of life. Her parents' efforts to help her manage her disabilities led them to a meeting with Alexander Graham Bell. Bell is best known for being awarded the U.S. patent for the first workable telephone, but it was his interest in speech and hearing (to assist his deaf mother and wife) that led him to develop the first generation of hearing devices. It was Bell's recommendation that eventually led Helen and her parents to Anne Sullivan. This amazing teacher was hugely instrumental in helping Helen overcome her bumps in the road and ultimately be able to communicate and function in the world.

In addition to learning how to speak, Helen was the first deaf and blind person to receive a bachelor's degree; she was a prolific author (authoring 12 books); she helped found the American Civil Liberties Union (ACLU), she founded her own organization devoted to research in vision and health, she was active in politics, met every U.S,

President from Grover Cleveland to Lyndon B Johnson, and became a world famous speaker, taking many trips overseas to share her wisdom with the world.

The lesson we can learn from Helen and why this story is such a great start to this book is that the difference between Helen and you is incredibly small. While Helen had tremendous support along her journey, it was through her own will and conviction, her attitude toward her bumps, that she was able to accomplish so much with her life by becoming an author, spokesperson, political advocate, and on and on....

You need to embrace the bumps in life. Don't let them slow you down. Do you think Helen sat around and held a pity party because she was blind and deaf? No. She was too busy enjoying her life (the journey), both the good and the bad. She was pursuing her dreams and aspirations, regardless of what got in her way. She treated these obstacles as exactly what they were...something to be navigated around in her exciting journey of life. Challenges along the way will happen and trying to avoid them is foolish. Embrace the bumps and enjoy the journey. Just like Helen Keller did...

Once your attitude is set for the positive, you are ready to start your journey in overcoming these obstacles. In the coming chapters, we will discuss the following challenges:

- Performance
- Failure
- Nemesis
- Create
- Crisis
- Personal Attack
- You

Each of these present a unique challenge for any leader, so let's dig in and learn how to overcome these challenges and pave your road to success.

Chapter 1 - Performance

Rose was the ultimate performer. Rose was an emergency room trauma surgeon. Her job was the embodiment of a pressure cooker, where every day people would come into her operating room with broken bones, head injuries, major blood loss, and any number of other life-threatening situations that she must fix. From the frantic 911 call of the incident, to the paramedics rushing the patients into the hospital, Rose constantly had to go from a state of calm to full on focus and concentration with the single goal of stabilizing and saving a person's life. Her patients have families and loved ones who are counting on Rose to perform at her best. Her job was truly life and death.

In social settings when meeting new people, Rose always received unusual reactions when telling people about her occupation. She normally got a fair dose of respect and admiration as even the uniformed know that an ER trauma doctor is a very difficult job. While the admiration and respect made her feel good about her vocation, more times than not, she also got a very unusual reaction.

New acquaintances would often ask Rose how she could do a job with so much loss, stress, and chaos. They felt sorry that she had to work long hours and oftentimes deliver the worst news to families about their loved ones who had passed away. Rose never understood why people looked at her job this way. Her job gave her life purpose. She was solely focused on savings lives and delivering people back to health and their families. The chaos and drama that encapsulated her world never really seemed to matter as she was so aligned with her purpose. People didn't understand the level of skill and confidence Rose had at her job and the satisfaction she got from doing it well. She spent years in med school, followed by a two-year fellowship and countless other specific studies and training to perfect her unbelievable skills. The years of preparation had built her confidence to a point where it was almost super natural. She believed every single patient brought into her operating room could be saved (and oftentimes were). After these social interactions, she was always left wondering, "Why don't people understand the importance of my job and my sense of purpose? Do they not have a similar sense of purpose in their life and possess the skills and confidence to do their job well?" Rose wondered what she was missing…

++++

I am a big fan of live music. Seeing a concert is something I really enjoy doing, especially with my wife. I have my list of favorite bands that I love, some new and some old, and am always on the lookout for when they are coming to my city. When you get to see a band play your favorite song live, it's just a totally different experience than listening to it on the album. You really can't tell how good a band is until you see them perform live and do their thing in front of an audience. Can they really perform, or are they just studio artists? One of my favorite concerts of all-time was a Jimmy Buffett concert I saw when I was 14-years-old. It was one of the first concerts I ever went to that was a decent band and without adult supervision (for the record, my first concert ever was the Grateful Dead with my grade school buddy... and his mom). I knew I really liked Jimmy's music, along with the Parrot Heads (the nickname for the devout followers of Buffet), but wasn't sure how much his songs would differ in the outdoor amphitheater where we went to see the show.

While I somewhat remember all the sights, sounds, and people, what really stuck with me was his performance. He was having so much fun and absolutely rocking the songs he had probably played a million times. The crowd was into it, I was into it, and the songs sounded twice as good as they did on his albums because there was

> Our ability to perform well, regardless of the circumstance, is key to our success in life.

so much energy in everyone around us. The experience was amazing and changed how I felt about music and what it meant to be a performer. Music wasn't only meant to be listened to through ear buds or headphones but experienced in an environment where it can be felt with all your senses. That performance made all the difference in my love for live music and changed how I felt about the world around me.

We have to perform in our lives every day. From the moment you turn on the lights in the morning and make breakfast for your family, to giving the sales pitch to the senior executive, it's all performance all the time. Our ability to perform well, regardless of the circumstance, is key to our success in life. To be a successful leader, we must perform well and mastering your performances is one of the major challenges you will face as a leader.

I define performance as the execution of a task within your daily life, the success or failure of which is determined by various factors. Merriam-Webster defines performance as "the execution of an action." A performance is *doing* something. And we do *something* many, many times throughout the day. Some might say each performance is different, based on its importance to us (i.e. driving to the grocery store vs. a sales presentation), but I argue that the only difference is how confident we are in delivering the performance. That's why rock stars, politicians, and entertainers are so intriguing to us because they can sing, act, and make speeches in front of thousands of people and not be fazed by it at all. They are in control of the situation and have a larger-than life persona. For the rock star, putting on the larger than life show is like flipping a switch. They are confident. They are in control. They are not scared. When delivering the sales pitch to the senior executive becomes as routine as flipping on a light switch, you are sure to become a rock star of the board room.

Some of us are very natural performers. High performers espouse several critical traits that allow them to perform a particular task exceptionally well. Any doubt that we have will manifest itself in our performances. Not every person is a natural born performer, in fact, I would say a great many of us are not even *good* performers. It's not in our nature. Not everyone can walk onto a NBA basketball court and drain a jumper in front of thousands of screaming fans and television cameras. Not everyone can fly a fighter jet moving at speeds that break the sound barrier and control it without pooping their pants. Not everyone can stand in front of their peers and deliver a motivational speech with high levels of confidence and swagger. Regardless of who we are or what we do, we all have to perform in our daily lives and there are three major traits to being a great performer. Most great performers possess:

- Confidence
- A sense of purpose
- Desire to perform well

Each of these traits plays a major role in how well we perform and are all traits we can learn and acquire over time. Some things we are born with but others we can learn through our own grit and determination. But before anything else, it all starts with confidence.

Confident to the Core

So you need confidence to perform well, but what is confidence really and where does it come from? Merriam-Webster defines confidence as "a feeling or belief that you can do something well." As the clinical definition indicates, confidence is tightly interwoven to performing. If we *don't* believe we can do something, then we are probably right! On the flip side of the coin, if we *do* believe we can do it, we are likely also right. I believe it was Confucius, the Chinese teacher and philosopher, who said, "The man who says he can and the man says he cannot are both usually right." But confidence is a funny thing. For some people, it is constantly there and present in their lives, while in others, it is fleeting and hard to find. Do any simple web search on confidence and performance and you'll see tons of articles from psychologists and other academics tightly tying these two things together. In my view, the people that perform the BEST are good because they have done it before and are prepared. They believe in themselves because they have done it before. That's right, *experience* and *preparation* are the building blocks of confidence. Figure those out and you will perform with confidence in all facets of your life, including even the most mundane tasks.

I am supremely confident I can turn on the light switch in my bedroom…and by golly, I am the best in the world at it! My wife? She's got nothing on me. I am *THE* best when it comes to turning on the bedroom lights. No one can deny it! This is a ridiculous example, of course, but it proves my point that I can perform this simple task with high levels of confidence mostly because I have done it a bunch (experience) and have a plan (preparation) on how to do it. No matter how many people are watching or how important it might be to my career, I am confident and relaxed when it comes to performing this simple task, hence my ability to do it so well. While seemingly trivial, simply having a plan of attack for your performance is immeasurably helpful and critical. It blows my mind how many people don't have a game plan for their big performances (presentation, interview, ball game, conversation with child, etc.). How can you ever develop confidence and perform well if you don't have a plan? As George Harrison once stated, "If you don't know where you're going, any road will take you there…"

I bet all of us can think of a time when we didn't plan and prepare correctly for a big performance and it didn't go well. The reason having a plan is so critical is that it is the map for getting to our desired outcome. If you don't have a plan, then you really have no way at all of knowing whether you have done a good job or not. It's vital. This is even more important for a task you have never performed before. I won't try to prescribe to you what your plan should be or include. That ultimately comes down to the individual, performance, and your desired outcome. What I will prescribe is that for those key performances, writing down your plan of attack will significantly up your likelihood for success.

There are lots of ways to prepare for your performance and one could write an entire book on that alone. The best way to prepare for a performance is specific to the person and situation, but what works for me is having a written plan or outline. I had to give a presentation on a technical topic (IT controls and data mining, yawn!) early in my career and was struggling on how to prepare and make it "pop" for the audience who were mostly my peers. It was important for me to do this presentation well, as I was early in my career and needed to display leadership, confidence, and demonstrate my ability to perform on a large stage (literally). I knew the content of what I wanted to say but wanted it to be good because the topic was sort of mundane (sort of?!). I decided to write an outline. By doing this, two great things happened. One, I could see the big picture of what I wanted to get across (my purpose… foreshadowing) on one sheet and it allowed me to re-tool the strategy and make it "flow" better. Second, it forced me to practice the flow and put the different pieces of the presentation together as one. Writing it down forced me to bring together the strategy and execution in one piece of paper. Same thing with my past marathons. I always had a written down training plan before I started training for any marathon which I would look at in totality (Enough rest? Enough speed work? Enough miles) and then adjust it once I actually started to execute on the plan. Writing it down really works for me. There's also something unique about the process of having to physically write it down that activates your brain and forces you to engage on the task at hand. I would argue that writing down your plan is so important that not doing it for critical performances will ensure they do not go well. The board presentation? Sales pitch? Ball game? School play? Having that plan to fall back on provides the clarity you need to execute and deliver. Without a written plan, you are basically winging it and most of us won't perform with confidence when winging it.

Another preparation tip that builds confidence for an important performance, especially in the business world, is having the performance *before* the actual performance. Well, what in the heck does that mean? Some people might call this the dress rehearsal. In my career, I have had several important sales meetings, parenting situations, or other key performances where there was going to be various parties involved and I knew the desired outcome was critical. In addition to being critical, the varying parties had different objectives and points of view that needed to be met. The varying needs were far too critical for me to put all my eggs in one basket and hope (pray) that we would accomplish what we wanted in the final performance. In those cases, I would essentially make time with each of the parties and go over the agenda and desired outcomes and expectations in advance of the actual performance. I communicated to them what I planned to say or have happen in the actual performance before it happened. Have the performance before the performance. It works very well. This makes the actual performance a piece of cake. Everyone is on the same page, and if there is dirty laundry to be aired or challenges to be encountered, you've already dealt with it because you performed it with everyone in advance. This also allows you to relax because it takes away as many of the unknowns as possible. This is why coaches develop a game plan with their team and walk through it prior to the actual game. It's why professionals will talk to key stakeholders before a board meeting or other critical discussion. I even did this successfully when talking to my daughter about getting her first cell phone. Talk about a tricky conversation. I had the conversation with my wife and then daughter laying out the ground rules getting feedback and input before we "formally" sat down and had the talk. It diffused some of the key sticking points when we sat down to discuss, and the conversation went much better than you could expect talking with a preteen about mobile phones and social media!

It's a totally different feeling when you walk into a meeting or performance and have no idea what to expect vs. walking into that same performance and you already know the outcome! What a great way to relieve the stress of the big performance and build your confidence. I find this hugely effective in sales pitches as well. If a client knows your price, knows what you bring to the table, and has shared any concerns, you are in a very favorable position going into the discussion and your confidence will be high. Always have the performance before the performance if you can. So, having a plan is key to success, huh? What about experience? Didn't I say experience was important for confidence as well?

I'll never forget one sales pitch I was making for a high-profile prospective client. I had a perfect game plan of what I wanted to say and every point I wanted to make was well thought out and written down. I had practiced what I was planning to say and felt very confident walking into the pitch because I was *prepared*. Then it came time for my big performance. The stakes for this sales pitch were high, as this was a potential new client and the revenue at stake was significant for our firm. Even though I had done this before, the enormity of it made it somehow… different. I was nervous. I have very high personal standards for my performances and was layering on more pressure than what was really needed. It was a team effort for our firm, but I couldn't shake the fact this was hugely important for my career and I worried that I would not do well and blow my chance. So instead of calming myself down and executing my plan, I let my nerves get the best of me, panicked, and delivered a sub-par performance. My lack of experience caused me to stutter on a few lines, make poor eye contact, and come off as amateur and nervous. I clearly lacked the experience for this big moment. Had I possessed several more under my belt, I would have calmed myself and easily delivered on my plan. But I didn't have that experience and basically trashed all the work I had done in advance. We didn't win the work (fortunately, not because of me, but because of a competitor's better bid), but I can't help but think that maybe I had something to do with the loss. Maybe they didn't see the confidence in my role that they needed? Maybe it was our price? Maybe it was something they just couldn't put their finger on. Regardless, I knew I didn't do my best solely because I wasn't able to relax and deliver with confidence like I wanted to.

While having a plan is key to developing confidence and performing at a high level, it isn't the only thing. Sometimes having the years of experience really helps bolster your confidence and deliver better. Even though I had this great plan for my sales pitch, when it came time to execute, I lacked the experience to really perform well. The good experiences, the bad experiences, and everything in between allow your confidence to build slowly over time. The best performers have many bad experiences over and over before they actually start to take small learnings from each failure and transition to a high performing Rockstar. The fantastic author, Malcolm Gladwell, suggested that it takes roughly 10,000 hours of practice (experience) before you can actually master a craft and become a high performer. So the bad news about experience is that it must be earned over time. There are no shortcuts. Period. The good news, however, for those reading this book is that you simply need to devise a solid plan and then develop yourself through lots of hard work, and viola, you'll be a professional and confident performer. For those of us that are too impatient to wait that long, don't fear. There are some ways around the lack of experience to get you what is needed to confidently perform at your best until you get those 10,000 hours.

When you are younger and lack experience in high-pressure situations, it seems overwhelming and surreal and the emotional overload results in a lack of focus and poor performance. After having these experiences over and over, learning from each mistake, the pressure of it starts to fade. Another huge reason we sometimes don't perform our best in certain situations has to do with the audience. Most of us would say that if we gave that speech, presented the sales pitch, shot the free throw or said the lines, without anyone around, we would perform most tasks very well. So what is it about having an audience that makes any difference at all? We've all seen it. The all-star who shines during warm-ups and practice and then seems to wilt once the lights come on. The smartest guy in the room until when it counts in the boardroom and something needs to be done in reality. The musician who can nail every single note of a song until the lights come on and the audience are in their seats and they fall apart. If you're reading this, it's probably happened to you on some level. If you are one of those people without lots of experience or lacking in confidence, sometimes you just have to fake it.

Ever heard of couch confidence? Just about everything you do on the couch, you do with extreme relaxation as if you have years of experience doing it. Watch TV. Read a book. Have a chat. Couch confidence is a way neutralize those situations where you don't have the 10,000 hours of experience and to not be distracted by the people and focus solely on the task. I apply this couch confidence to areas where I lack experience and not performing to the level I think I should be. The question I ask myself is, "How would I perform this task if I was sitting at home on my couch?" This is another way of asking how you would perform this task if you were comfortable… if you had years of experience. With no one around you to watch and judge you, how confident would you be in performing this task? People watching us perform don't have mind control over us, yet their mere presence changes everything about the performance and blurs our focus. Some might say that you'll never perform a sales pitch on your couch or nail the winning free throw on you couch, but it's meant to provide perspective and build confidence where experience is lacking. Envisioning your performance as if you are delivering it on the couch, with no one around, also creates a silly visual that helps relax you during the actual performance. If you think about it simply, the things preventing us from performing well are very small and petty when you strip away all the noise. Typically, the only thing preventing us from performing at a high level is inside our head!

Still suffering from a lack of confidence and limited experience? There's another way for you to work with the fact that you may not have the 10,000 hours of experience yet. For the longest time, people always called me "likeable," and whenever I heard that, I always cringed. It seemed like the person praising me didn't have enough tangible good things to say about me or my skillset, so they gave me this back-handed compliment. It took me a long time to realize that having charisma was a pretty awesome trait to have. You

> ...never underestimate the power of charisma.

should never underestimate the power of charisma. Charisma provides an air of confidence and mastery when one might not really exist. Not everyone has that. Many people stick with the stupid Godfather line of "it's not personal, it's business." I hate that line because it just isn't reality. Making things personal with the people you interact with and making a connection with them is not something that everybody does. In addition, I have been around enough professionals and organizations to know that folks who have charisma and provide an air of positivity are sometimes hard to find. I like knowing about people and their stories; it's interesting to me. People love to talk about themselves and their lives and I like to hear about it. Those two things allow for an easy connection to be made and for people to see me as likeable.

So what does charisma have to do with performing and confidence? A lot. If someone likes you, they are more apt to help you out and look past your shortcomings. People gravitate to those with confidence. Charisma also helps you stick out and get more opportunities. Charisma is that little extra thoughtfulness you sprinkle in while performing the task that shows a level of mastery and builds confidence in the audience. It helps them to better hear your message and "fake it" when it comes to your lack of experience. Being liked and having charisma should never be a crutch, but it will definitely buy you a "hall pass" here and there and will also make it more likely that you will be provided with honest feedback, which is critical to growth. Throwing in some humor and charm goes a long way. So very few people use charisma beyond trying to find a mate and are not utilizing a valuable life skill. I read an article recently that said Marlon Brando was the number one most charismatic celebrity beating out the likes of Michael Jackson and Bob Dylan. One of Brando's most famous quotes was "Don't mistake the size of your paycheck for the size of your talent." Just like Brando leveraged his unique charm and charisma to excel on the silver screen, so can you become likeable very quickly if you show charisma or humor that relaxes your audience and puts them at ease. In most cases, the audience wants to see the performer succeed and do well. No one wants to see someone presenting who is nervous, and showing a little charisma can go a long way to get the audience to like you and be on your side. I am not telling you to kiss rear-ends or not deliver a difficult message. Quite the opposite. Having some charm and charisma can help you quite a bit in your leadership journey and it is an over-looked aspect of performance that many skip over because they are nervous or focused too much on the details.

Confidence is critical to any performance. The foundation of confidence is experience, having a plan, and believing in yourself. There are ways to compensate for lack of confidence but having it is critical to your success as a performer. While confidence is the key, having a purpose is also paramount to your success as a leader and performer.

Do it on Purpose
What are some of the best performances you can remember in your lifetime? Sir Anthony Hopkins dramatic portrayal of Hannibal Lector in the movie, *The Silence of the Lambs*? How about Michael Jordan's 38-point performance in the 1997 NBA finals against the Utah Jazz

when he had the stomach flu? The U.S. and Allied troops storming the beaches at Normandy, France during WWII and turning the tide of the war? What about the lifetime performance of Mother Theresa devoting herself to the poor and needy in India? All of these are amazing performances that were done at an incredibly high level, despite encountering difficulties along the way. Each of these performers had a very high sense of purpose around what they were doing, and each performance is amazing in its own way (physical, spiritual, bravery, emotional, etc.). Whether it was feeding poor people, winning the big game, depicting a complex character through acting, or something in between, each performer had a high sense of purpose and vision around what they wanted to do with fear of failure likely being a complete afterthought. While purpose can really drive optimal performance, it can also apply undue stress and erode your performance.

Not all of us can tie our performances to something so deeply ingrained in the fiber of our being the way Mother Theresa, Michael Jordan, or Sir Anthony Hopkins did, but we can bring ourselves to a similar state of calmness and focus that allows us to do our task and do it with purpose. Think of a great performance you have witnessed. Was that person nervous or scared? Perhaps. Did they believe in themselves enough to overcome that and do their best? Absolutely. Trying to relax myself helps get me aligned with my sense of purpose. Before a big performance, I might put on soothing music or breathe very slowly in through my nose and out through my mouth. Trying to keep myself calm before I perform, I also think about my purpose in the performance. When I have a reason for wanting to succeed, it clarifies why performing my best is so important and it motivates me.

What is purpose anyway and what does it have to do with performing? Merriam-Webster defines purpose as "something set up as the reason why something is done or created." Very simply, it is your reason for being. It is the reason you were put on this earth. It's your mission statement and *typically* lines up with your natural abilities. It's something the guys at F3 Nation (www.F3nation.com) call merging your Dolphin and Daffodil. When you can tie a performance or a task to something so personal, so close to you, it makes your purpose come to life and drives excellence. It's sometimes difficult to determine your purpose. People search their whole lives for their purpose in life and try to figure out why they are put on this earth. I always thought my purpose was providing for my family and protecting them. That is a great thing, of course, but it's really something I feel an obligation to do more than my purpose. I then flopped thinking my purpose was my job. Mostly because I do it so much of the day. Something I do all day and every day should be my purpose, right? Well, maybe eventually that could be the case, but for most people, that just isn't reality. After lots of searching and reflection, I finally figured out my purpose and that was the genesis of this book. It's best to tell a story…

I was very nervous during my last job interview. I was worried whether interviewing for this job was the right move for my family (and me), as I was leaving a place of comfort and stability. I was also at a time in my life where I finally felt clear on my purpose in life. This new job would allow me to provide for my family, yes, but it was also much more than that. I had come to point in my life where I knew my purpose was around serving others. Helping them, teaching them, motivating them to do better, and overcome their own obstacles in life. I had suffered through my own personal challenges but had come out on the other side a new man. I also possessed the God-given ability and leadership skills to help others overcome their own challenges. So, there I sat in my car, just minutes before this job interview, and I was nervous that I had made a big mistake. I had practiced my interview responses the days before and reviewed my resume in detail but felt I was leaving a place of comfort and stability. Eventually, my thoughts wondered to my purpose. Why am I here? As I tried to calm myself, I thought about my family and how this opportunity, while a move from my comfort zone, was a way to better provide for them. I also thought about the freedom this job would allow and provide more time to finish this book and then mentor those that were struggling. I *needed* to perform well for all of them. I didn't practice my responses any further but simply relaxed for the remaining ten minutes before walking in. No further prep, just serenity and extreme focus on my purpose for this performance. It was bigger than me. This took my heart rate way down and got me to a position of focus and confidence. Guess what happened? I nailed the interview. I nailed it because I was calm and focused on my purpose.

Another thing most people forget is that the stakes of our performances are the highest to… us. Sometimes an acute awareness of our purpose can put undue pressure on ourselves. In reality, the others witnessing the performance really don't care. Or at least not as much as you. They are not sitting there waiting to critique your every move. They are not nitpicking your clothes, your mannerisms, your idiosyncrasies, although sometimes this can happen (see the Chapter on Personal Attacks). They want your best performance; they aren't there to judge a beauty contest. Point being is that sometimes a great performance can be one devoid of major flaws or missteps. It doesn't have to be where you come in and set the room on fire or walk on water. Simply getting through the performance clean and easy is sometimes the best way to go. Now, I would never suggest to do anything mediocre. Everyone should do their best in any circumstance and all the preparation, practice, and relaxation mentioned in this chapter should be applied on all important performances. But in some cases, your performance doesn't require more than checking the box and completing the task. No frills, no fireworks, just getting it done. When the stakes are low and the attendees basically know the outcome, then getting in and out is acceptable. Sometimes a no frills, check the box performance is acceptable and what is needed for the situation. Always strive for the best, but know that in some cases, getting by with no hiccups is a success.

Putting pressure on yourself or making the issue bigger than it really is will lead to undue stress and diminished performance. Sometimes you can have too much purpose! I had one Mentee who was having a hard time at work and was visibly stressed out. He was so focused on the infinite tasks that needed to get done and the perceptions of his manager that it was causing the quality of work to go down. It was eating him alive. He visibly looked tired, his quality of work had suffered, and his demeanor toward others was short and grumpy. His purpose was eroding his performance and what he really needed was a dose of IDGAF. What is IDGAF, you ask? I pronounce it *ID-gaf* and it stands for *I Don't Give A Flip*. This is a change in mindset where you focus on what you can control vs. outcomes. Instead of stressing out about the outcome (Will I get the sale? Will I sink the shot?), you hone in on your effort and attitude around the performance which in turn drives the right outcomes.

I took this employee aside and told him about IDGAF and what it represented. Sometimes for effect, I'll change the final "F" in IDGAF to something a little more attention-grabbing then "flip." I did that with this person to break the ice and he kind of laughed at first, but this look of understanding came over his face. He realized he was pressing too much and making a tough situation even worse. Relaxing a little bit and not being so focused on the outcome (purpose) allowed him to relax more and his confidence went back up along with his performance. It was a simple thing but yielded big value in his performance. I, too, have found myself in a situation where I needed a huge dose of IDGAF. Instead of working myself up, I needed to say, "To heck with it, I'll do my best and whatever happens, happens." Mark Manson wrote an excellent book on this topic and I highly recommend you pick up. It is truly an art form and one that requires deep exploration.

The good news is if you are a person who falls into the IDGAF trap every once in a while, that means you truly care and want to own the quality of your performances and you do have a high sense of purpose. You care. Believe me, this is not a quality everyone has, and you should be proud of yourself that you're one of the few who really wants to do their best and take pride in your work. Employers out there want as many of these people working for them as possible. These people own their work and are personally invested in doing well. While this is a great trait to have, sometimes these people need to take a dose of IDGAF to keep their sanity. It really is ok to do this every once in a while. I would not suggest doing it all the time, but in moderation, it is okay to drop your guard and say "screw it," especially when you really look at the situation and know that's what is needed.

On the flip side, I've seen others who live in a perpetual state of IDGAF. They have no purpose, and therefore, they are not high performers. This is not good either. Some people can pull off this super relaxed carefree attitude and be successful, but I haven't seen many that lasted long in the professional world. If you are one of the permanently IDGAF folks, dialing up the amount you care and your intensity will help drive quality and accountability into your life. The reality is that even in stressful work situations, no one is sick and dying and the world won't end because of your upcoming performance (unless maybe you're a soldier, brain surgeon, or heart doctor!). If you find yourself a little stressed and over-preparing for the big performance, stop and give yourself a dose of IDGAF. It will help you when it counts.

A final interesting thought on purpose and performance is related to your wingman. If you've seen the movie *Top Gun*, you know the value of a wingman. Someone who is there by your side, plays a supporting role, and can help you when things get dicey. They also typically share a similar purpose for why they try to perform at their best. Having a wingman in critical performances brings you a sense of comfort and support knowing you have someone there who can chip in and contribute if you need it. In many cases, you may not need this person, but I find even if they don't actively contribute on your performance, having them there to help read the audience, provide feedback on what you could do better, or to simply being an active listener is tremendously helpful for your big performances. Some of the great duos of all time had a wingman. Batman had Robin. Jordan had Pippen. Maverick had Goose. Salt had Peppa. Many people don't leverage the wingman because they want to get the "credit" for whatever it is they are doing and figure having someone else there diminishes that in some way (this happens in sales all the time). Or they think the person may not lend anything to the conversation. Even still some people think it as a sign of weakness. All couldn't be further from the truth. Having that person in the performance will in most cases do the opposite of what some people perceive will happen. Also, most people do not like meeting someone new alone, and having a wing-man there can be a good way to break the ice or allow the more familiar parties to catch-up. In all cases, if the person does nothing other than listen, it was worth having them there.

A fresh and new perspective can help you question assumptions and ensure the performance is a rich and valuable experience. The old adage that two heads are better than one certainly applies here. Since people think and process information so differently, it really is beneficial to have someone there with you during your performance. A great example is on one of my former teams at work. I hired this person who was totally different from me as I felt they brought a totally new perspective to my team. I would always bring them to my key meetings and made sure they had an active role and the "green-light" to speak up in the meeting. This always brought a unique and different perspective than I could bring by myself. In team sports, this is super critical in order to be efficient and effective. Just like the point guard and other scorers on the team need to be in sync to pass the ball and get themselves in good position to score, so do team members in the professional setting. Coaches have assistant coaches for this very reason as everyone has a different role to play or perspective to bring. Having that other person to bounce ideas off or help you during the performance is a no-brainer way to put your absolute best foot forward. For those that aren't taking advantage of the wingman, why not? Explore why you may not be doing that and be honest with yourself. Maybe just don't even think about it. Or you might have deep-rooted reasons buried somewhere deep down in your subconscious that you don't even realize. Regardless, I ask you to closely explore why this is the case. Take a chance and include someone in your next big performance. Whether it's the planning component or the actual execution, you'll be delightfully surprised at how helpful and uplifting it is to include someone else in the important moments of your life.

Those of you with significant others should always include your partner in some way. This person knows you very well and will give you the most honest advice and guidance. In addition to that, being open and sharing with your significant other will bring the two of you closer together, which helps all elements of your life together. Those that don't share with their spouse are missing out on a huge opportunity to bring them closer to you in all facets of your life.

The best thing about a wingman is that bringing them with you to these performances is also an amazing way for them to learn as well. Seeing someone more senior, or with a different perspective and style, is a great opportunity for the wingman to learn how to operate in those situations. It's a win-win for everyone. If you really want to have your mind blown think about this: What if your wingman is Michael Jordan? Not literally, but what if your wingman is the best at something? Pass him the ball, dummy! If you want to be successful, then sometimes giving your wingman some big responsibilities is a great solution as well. Whatever the circumstance, I challenge you to bring someone into your next big performance. The value of their interaction will be very impactful and helpful beyond your expectations.

Object of Your Desire

I believe most of us have lying inside us the best version of ourselves. That version of ourselves is amazing and powerful, is not scared of anything, and can perform tasks that our real self could never dream of doing. Through our upbringing or our experiences in life, that amazing person gets shaped and formed into a diluted version of the you *you* are today. It's not bad or wrong, but it's just human nature that causes us to build up walls of self-preservation (see the You chapter). These walls prevent us from performing certain tasks to the best of our ability. We will never fully know all the reasons why we are what we are today (nature, nurture, or everything in between), but let's explore how we can move past the barriers we put upon ourselves during our most critical performances. The best ways to knock down these walls and perform at your peak is through your desire.

Do you accept opportunities to take on challenging or new performances? Or maybe you're the person that shrinks away from those opportunities? Are you sitting on the sidelines? You may have read the words from this chapter and arrived at the conclusion that you are a magnificent performer. But if you have never failed a performance or taken a big risk, then you likely are not a good performer at all but someone who is fooling themselves. This lack of taking on the challenging performances might be holding you back in life. I find many people lack the desire to succeed. Think about that. Many people don't *want* to perform well. Staying in your cone of safety is comfortable and void of any risk. Desire is defined as the feeling of wanting something. Most of us desire success on a basic level but aren't willing to take on the risk to achieve it. I'm not suggesting everyone should take on major risk, but everyone *should* take small chances to help push their comfort zone and grow. You'll be surprised at what you are capable of with the right level of desire for risk. So tell me honestly, do you ever take on any risks?

Most of us who grew up in the 80's know the iconic movies *Pretty in Pink* and *The Breakfast Club*. These movies were about coming of age and the growing pains we all experience in high school around relationships and the joys of puberty. These movies really captured the spirit of growing up in middle-class America, and at the center of these iconic flicks was the actor Molly Ringwald. She was the un-assuming redhead who was the focal point of these movies. For a period, no Hollywood star shone brighter in the 80's than Molly. While we all know her for these iconic roles, some may not know that she passed over a huge role in her career. While Molly is associated with these blockbuster movies, Julia Roberts is also associated with an iconic movie of her own, *Pretty Woman*. *Pretty Woman* was a somewhat controversial film depicting an unusual relationship between a prostitute and millionaire businessman played by Richard Gere. Allegedly Molly was offered this role and turned it down, as she wasn't too keen on playing a prostitute and tarnishing her all-American status from her previous roles. While Molly purportedly passed on this controversial role, Julia Roberts decided to roll the dice and take on this risky character. Not only did Julia take the role, she nailed the performance, receiving an Academy Award nomination for best actress and it catapulted her career to the next level of stardom where she has become a Hollywood star and icon for decades. Meanwhile, Molly somewhat faded into the background, taking on lesser roles in film and television. There may be other reasons, but you could certainly argue that not taking the risk of this new and different role hurt her career in the end. We will never know for sure, but the lesson here is to not get complacent and continue to challenge yourself and take on risky performances proving you desire success!

This is your call to think about the times you have sat there and looked the other way when there was a need to have someone stand up and perform for your team/family. Have you passed up one of those opportunities because it was too risky or hard? It's okay if you have, but slow down and think through those opportunities if they arise again. Never feel like you need to do this alone either. Enlisting someone to help can be valuable in so many ways and can take some of the pressure off of you to take on more as you learn and grow. The bottom line is you shouldn't go it alone and you definitely shouldn't miss out on opportunities to perform based on fear and not taking any risks. Don't sit on the sidelines and don't pass up these opportunities to perform.

I am a big substance-over-form guy. To the core. Meaning I value results over simply looking good. I have come across far too many people who are more concerned over how they look vs. what they accomplish. Most of the time these folks lack a desire to succeed and value petty things, like vanity, safety. Performing well will allow you to *accomplish* things with confidence, poise, passion, and conviction. Can you achieve your stated goal (whatever it may be) without passion, conviction, confidence, poise, or desire? No. Or at the very least, it becomes exponentially more difficult without those things. If people are to look up to you as a leader in your home, work, church, or otherwise they want to have that warm and fuzzy feeling that you are in control and an intelligent person. Right, wrong, or indifferent, sometimes how you perform will impact people's perception of you. People *need* leaders to follow. How you perform paints other people's picture of you, and if you come off as uncertain, nervous, or small, it can make it difficult for people to rally behind you. If you don't have a strong desire to lead and perform, those who are supposed to follow you can tell. I promise...

Why else does a stellar performance matter? We live in a world where we have to perform to survive. It seems dramatic, but it's the truth. Going back to when we were cavemen, the ones who performed well on the hunt were the ones that ate and survived. Those that didn't starved and got eaten by a sabre tooth tiger. Ok, a little dramatic I know, but you get the point. Our world has evolved just a bit since caveman times, but some of the principles are still very much the same. Perform at your job and you put a roof over your head and food on the table. Don't perform well and see what happens. It's a pretty simple correlation to how well you perform at work and your ability to bring home the bacon. Point being, performing well at whatever it is we do is paramount to our well-being and the livelihood of our families. There are essentially no jobs today that don't involve some form of a performance review. Your grade on this review correlates to raises, bonuses, and promotions. Did you improve during the review period?

Did you digress? What sets you apart from your peer group? Performance, performance, performance. If you're still not a believer in how important it is to perform well, try not performing at all. You'll see how quickly you get shown the door if you just stop performing your job!

Some people may be fully on board with the notion that performing at your best is key to your success. But what about those that just feel like they simply aren't getting a chance to show all they can do? Those folks that are ready to step up to the plate, but something is preventing them from getting opportunities to perform. They have the purpose and desire, they have the preparation and are relaxed and focused on what needs to happen but simply aren't getting a chance to "strut their stuff." Unfortunately, this is a situation many of us find ourselves in. We know we have the right stuff, but even after asking for opportunities, nothing seems to materialize. Or perhaps our job just doesn't warrant or allow for opportunities to make it count.

Even if you're not getting the big opportunities, there are still chances to show what you can do through many smaller interactions. All performances count, even the small ones. It's a simple example, but my best "small" performance was a parenting moment. The whole family was at the pool and the kids were off doing their thing and the parents were hanging out doing ours. As I was having a great conversation with one of my buddies, my son, who was five-years-old at the time, walked up to me asking for candy from the snack bar. I told him no, he had enough already from earlier that day. He immediately started crying and whining about how he wanted it and how I was mean for not letting him have it. He threw a total fit. As parents, we've all been there before, and when it's your kid, it's embarrassing and you feel it reflects poorly on you. I told him very firmly, but calmly, that I was not talking to him until he settled down and got himself together. I stood there solemnly while he tried to calm himself. Waiting.

Waiting. It took him about two full minutes, but he finally got there. I forced him to ask his question again, but this time, without crying or whining. I explained to him calmly that he could not have any more candy *today*, but if behaved for the rest of the night and tomorrow, he could get a treat if he *earned* it. To this day, he knows that crying and whining isn't getting him anywhere and that our decisions as parents were final.

I got several compliments from my buddies, also dads, on how I handled that situation. Instead of getting mad, I forced myself to handle it correctly to make the point. It was a small performance, but it had a big impact. Even the small performances count and will be a big factor in how well you perform as a leader at your job, home, church, or rec league basketball team. Any good leader or boss will respect excellence, regardless of the size of the task. If you aren't getting big chances to shine, treat those smaller performances on the same level as the larger ones as it will show what you can do on larger scale. Also, sometimes if you aren't getting chances to perform, you have to make your chances. This all comes from desire. If you have the desire, do it anyway.

If you ask to balance your department budget and the boss says he doesn't need the help, do it anyway. Make a spreadsheet showing the variances and bring it to your boss each month with suggestions on how to resolve. If you ask the regional sales manager to be part of a big sales pitch and he says no, offer to go and take notes to learn and build relationships with the other team members. If you aren't getting staffed on the good projects, don't whine. Setup a meeting with the partner and plead your case to get assigned to the project even for a more junior role. Don't make excuses, make your desire to succeed known to everyone and you'll get plenty of chances.

What if, even despite excellence on the smaller scale performances, you are still not going where you want to go? I always encourage patience in these circumstances but also recognize that even the most patient person needs to consider alternatives if you are truly not getting enough opportunities. If you are one of those folks who has toiled within an organization and provided exceptional performance over a period and not seen any results, then perhaps a stellar performance in a job interview is what is really needed. I always view this as a last resort mostly because it feels like running away to me. However, I know in some cases you need to step out of an organization to get the opportunities you need. In any leadership role I've ever had (coach, parent, professional, etc.), I've always looked for three things:

1. Ability to work with good people
2. Challenging and exciting work
3. The opportunity to succeed and grow

Without one of the three items above, I know I am not in the right position for long-term success. In fact, I would argue that number three above is the most important. If you don't have opportunities for growth and success, then you are essentially stuck in a no-win leadership role and should explore other opportunities. Use your desire to create opportunities where you can, but don't be scared to create performance opportunities at another company or situation.

In Summary

We all have to perform in our daily lives. Our lives are filled with many different types of performances that are critical to our success. Doing those tasks that we need to do each day and doing them well is extremely critical to our success in whatever field or personal endeavor that we choose to embark upon. We should always strive to do our best, regardless of the situation, and several tools can help us do those things and do them well. Consciously thinking about the performance and taking small steps to prepare and relax will align our purpose and make all the difference in how well you perform. Challenge yourself and make it a priority, and you'll see the difference in those performances that matter most.

LTF Action Plan

1. Write down your plan for something small
2. Get 10,000 hours in something
3. Do IDGAF once a week
4. Create a new opportunity at work / home

Chapter 2 - Failure

Ken was a failure. At the age of 25, he had tried to start an online company specializing in financial money management, and after three years of trying to make it work, it had failed. By all accounts, Ken came from a very successful family. His father worked for the same large corporation for 35 years and provided a comfortable living for his family with memberships to the country club and private schools for Ken and his siblings. Ken's older brother attended an Ivy League school and was following the same path as their father as in-house legal counsel for an international paper company, living in Los Angeles. Ken's younger sister attended a top fashion and design school in Paris and now lived in New York where she was working as a designer for an elite clothing brand. Most impressive of all was Ken's mother, who was a former Rhodes Scholar and now author penning multiple best-selling historical fiction books about an Indiana Jones-type character. Ken's family was wildly successful.

Ken's failure was nagging at him almost daily. He had taken the traditional path in his studies like the rest of his family but wanted to try some-

thing different upon graduation. Ken eschewed the normal career path of taking an entry-level position and instead tried his hand at doing something different. He started this company leveraging his undergrad studies in computer science along with his post graduate education (MBA) in Finance. This startup was a more risky endeavor and forced him to constantly adapt his skill sets and learn new things. He owned all the outcomes of the company working tirelessly in the initial years playing a role in all major decisions. He learned more about life and business in the first three years with his startup than his father had learned in an entire career as a lawyer. Despite all of these good, practical lessons, he could not shake the feeling that he was a failure. He spent a lot of time reflecting on his failed business, but one question still remained. What was he going to do next? He gained all these great experiences and knowledge and felt he shouldn't just waste them and do something "normal,"? Was he going to go the traditional route like his family or was he going to apply what he learned and try again? Most importantly, would he learn from his failure and make the next outcome different?

++++

Stuff happens. And I know for me personally, "it" happens a lot. A whole bunch of the time "it" is my own fault as well. Everybody makes mistakes. We all know that as a truth of life. "To err is human, to forgive is divine," as the English poet Alexander Pope so eloquently wrote. Since you are a human reading this book (sorry to the intergalactic aliens out there), you have surely made a mistake at some point in your life. Some of you may have even made some epic mistakes along the way. Maybe it was dumping that girlfriend in high school who turned out to be the Oscar-winning actor or Nobel Prize winning scientist. Or maybe you sold that winning stock before it took off and made millions. Perhaps you put your foot in your mouth during an important meeting or flubbed a formula on an important spreadsheet. Did you call the wrong play for your kids' basketball team that cost them the game? Miss the winning shot? Or the worst mistake you can make – an error on your tax return! Gasp. Oh no!

All kidding aside, no one is perfect. But how many of us have *failed* at something? A failure sounds so terrible, but isn't a mistake the same thing as a failure? Nope, not really. Those are two totally different things. A mistake is when you did something wrong unintentionally or when you made an error. A mistake is when you add a number incorrectly or forget to put on your turn signal when merging onto the interstate. A mistake is something you can fairly easily recover from. A *failure* happens when you are personally vested in something, want it to succeed, and it *doesn't*. You work hard at a job you love, but your team is unsuccessful and you get fired for poor results. You start a fledgling technology company and pour your heart and soul into the success of the company and it goes bankrupt. Or if you're the Buffalo Bills' organization who pulled together a championship organization for years and years and failed at winning the Super Bowl three times (in a row). Or when you train tirelessly for years and run seven marathons trying to qualify for the Boston Marathon and do not make it (that would be me). A failure is something you are emotionally invested in, want to succeed, and simply do not. And it stings really, really bad.

I've been there. I trained for seven marathons, each one with the same goal in mind: qualifying for the Boston Marathon. Countless early mornings and long runs all preparing for a singular goal which was not achieved. Everyone would tell me how great of an accomplishment it was to simply *finish* the race…but in my mind, I had failed. I will admit I had a warped sense of reality on this goal and the sacrifice it would take to accomplish it. In every race, there would be a point where I simply mathematically could not get the time I needed to meet my goal and would literally almost start to cry. So much training, so much pain and time away from my family not to make my goal. But it was this failure that ultimately helped me get over a major life hurdle and help me deal with and avoid other failures in my life. Having suffered through those seven failures, I

> ...from each failure is a powerful lesson if you are willing to look and listen.

knew in my heart that I had not trained to my fullest potential. It was this realization that helped me understand that from each failure is a powerful lesson if you are willing to look and listen.

If you're a leader in your workplace or at home, you've had to deal with a failure at some point. Whether it be directly or indirectly, you've had to deal with it. I think failure isn't necessarily bad but for those who have been through one may tend to disagree. I would never suggest that the next few pages have some magical advice or insight on how to eliminate failures from your life. No words or insight can prevent anyone from failing, but as we'll discuss, there are ways to deal with failures, and sometimes failures aren't always a bad thing.

Most people see failure as the opposite of success. So, what then is success? Success is the accomplishment of an aim or purpose, or as Merriam-Webster defines it, "a degree or measure of succeeding." Could that be any vaguer? I think we all know what success looks and feels like on some level. Maybe you haven't climbed to the top of Mount Everest or started a billion-dollar business, but we've all had our own little successes along the way. Acing a test, making a team, the parental teaching moment, the excellent sales pitch, or the successful fundraiser... When we set out to do something meaningful and we accomplish it, it feels good. When we set out to do something meaningful and we fail, it feels absolutely awful.

In some professions, failing 60% of the time can establish you as one of the best. Take baseball for example. The highest lifetime career batting average is held by Ty Cobb and it is .3664. That means that 63.4% of the time, he failed to get a hit of any kind. 63% of the time, he failed! Now hitting a 90 mile-per-hour fast-

> So sometimes failure is relative, but in our minds, we treat all failures the same

ball is not an easy thing to do, so successfully doing that only 36% of the time really isn't so bad. In fact, it's the best of all-time! Michael Jordan is arguably the best basketball player ever to touch a basketball, and he had a field goal percentage of just under 50%. Under 50%! He made less than half his shots and is widely known as the best player to ever play the game. Again, making shots against some of the most athletic players in the world is not something that is easy to do, and scoring lots of points and winning championships doesn't hurt your case either. Larry Bird and Magic Johnson are also considered some of the greatest players to ever play the game. They both made around 50% of the shots they took for their entire career (although Magic is a tad over Michael in this department, at 52% for his career). So sometimes failure is relative, but in our minds, we treat all failures the same. Should we treat our failure to walk the dog the same as our failure to pay a bill or be successful at our job? The answer is no, but sometimes we feel the same amount of guilt and sorrow for failures that are not even on the same playing field.

My point here is that people can blur the lines between the words "fail" and "failure." They are very different words but many times used synonymously. Fail is "to be unsuccessful in achieving one's goal." The word fail is a verb and can also mean "to neglect to do something." Fail is not an adjective describing who you are as a person. On the other hand, the word failure is a noun. It is someone (or something) that lacks success. Many times we think if we fail at something, then we are a failure in general, but that couldn't be further from the truth. In fact, some of the people I know who have failed more times than you can imagine are in fact also the biggest successes I know. They may have failed and failed and failed and failed, yet they are not *failures*. In fact, they are all over your TV, social media, and in the headlines making news about their success...

Did you hear about the 22-year-old news anchor in Baltimore who was fired from one of her first TV co-anchoring jobs; executives said she was unfit for TV. She took that failure and subsequently launched her own talk show and turned that show into a launching pad for a multi-billion-dollar media empire: Oprah. What about the high school basketball player who was cut from his junior varsity team but then turned that failure into motivation, pushing him to make the varsity team go off to an elite college basketball program, win an NCAA national championship, win a gold medal, and go on to the NBA and become one of the most decorated and accomplished players in the history of basketball: Michael Jordan. Or the English teacher who had his first novel rejected 30 times before finally getting it published. This spring-boarded his writing career, leading to over 300 million copies of his books being sold worldwide: Stephen King. How about the tech executive who founded a company and helped lead it to success and then was fired from that same company later to be re-hired and lead it back to prominence: Steve Jobs.

You've probably heard of many of these people and know them as very successful celebrities, but the reality is they all failed at some point in their life. They are no different than any of us. What makes them different is they did not stop trying to pursue their goals and were willing to put themselves out there and not be afraid to fail. Quitting probably didn't even occur to them. In fact, you could even argue that their failures were a big factor in what resulted in them ultimately being successful. Failures are a complicated thing. As leaders we can learn from failures where we really tried our best but came up short. What we want to try to avoid are those *unnecessary* failures. Those failures where we don't try our best or maybe took a shortcut here and there. Those are stupid failures – don't make those. In general, however, I believe whether you make a meaningful failure or an unnecessary failure comes down to five things:

- Taking risk
- Balance
- Ownership
- Simplicity
- Doubt

All of these factors will determine whether your failures bring out the best in you or torture you throughout your life. Your inability to learn from your failures will seriously inhibit your ability to be a great leader regardless of the situation. In order to fail, though, you have to first take some risks.

Risky Business
Success is risky business. In order to lead any kind of fulfilling life, you have to take risks. Leading a life where you never experience failure would be shallow and listless because there is no better way to learn, grow, and lead than through your failures. Some people call it the school of hard knocks, but it's really just life in general. You learn from your failures just in the same way an infant learns how to walk

after falling repeatedly. What keeps those babies getting up over and over again after all those falls? Besides a short attention span, it's the excitement of what they can do once they can walk! Act like their older sibling? Grab that shiny object off the shelf? Or the excitement of doing something new and different and the resulting sense of accomplishment. Failure doesn't even cross their mind! You cannot succeed unless you have failed first and you cannot fail unless you take risk. Taking risk equates to success, which is the opposite of failure! The core thing to remember here is that failure is *good*. It's not bad. Failure is how you learn and grow. If you do not take any risks in your life, job, and family, then you will never fail and in turn experience very little success. But how do you know how much risk is the right amount? Unfortunately, it's never easy...

Take for example, my good friend Jason. Jason had been chasing his dream job ever since we first met. It was basically the same job he had then, sales rep, but he wanted to work for *the* company in his industry. Higher pay, more respect, better benefits, and the clients he always dreamed of. He tried and failed repeatedly to get a job at this company. Different level, different region, different boss. He tried almost anything to get into his dream job and he took some pretty serious risks along the way (Note: My dream job, centerfield for the New York Yankees is currently unavailable). Jason even went so far as to jump to another company, which he thought would position him for his dream job at the other company. After taking this transitional job for about six months, he was laid off. Laid off! He had a wife and two young kids at home and was now jobless all due to chasing his dream. On some level, he felt like he had failed as he confided in me about not knowing what to do. He was so steadfast in trying to achieve his goal that he stepped over a few lesser jobs while unemployed in the hope of landing his dream job. Talk about taking a risk! After all his persistence, heartache, and risks, he finally did land his dream job… and it was all that it was cracked up to be. It was worth the risk, and above all else, Jason had something that is difficult for many to even comprehend…faith.

Faith is a fascinating thing. Many associate it with the belief in God or the doctrines of a religion, but for this book, it is that but also the complete trust and confidence in someone or something. Faith is the ultimate risk repellant. It doesn't make risk go away but rather allows you to face risk head on because you believe you can overcome it. You believe you can succeed. You believe in yourself to succeed more so than any external risk factors that *could* interrupt your path. Every NFL quarterback has a risk that the next pass attempt could lead to an interception or incomplete pass. The elite quarterbacks have this overwhelming confidence that when they step onto the field nothing can stop them. Their job is very risky. Risk of injury. Risk of loss. Risk of interception. Risk of incomplete passes. You name it, there are lots of ways things can go bad for an NFL QB. QB's like Tom Brady, Joe Montana, Aaron Rodgers, and Joe Namath had a strong faith and belief in their teams and themselves to overcome the odds and to become champions. If my friend Jason had not believed in his vision, his mission, and ultimately his God-given abilities, he would never have taken on the risk to wait for the perfect job. In addition to my friend Jason, there are others you would recognize who have taken on risk.

The story of Walt Disney always fascinates me. Most know the stories of how Mickey, Minnie, Donald, Pluto, and Goofy came to be but most don't know the story of how Walt funded the Walt Disney Land theme park back in the 1950's. He effectively mortgaged every nickel of his personal wealth to help seed fund the park and start construction. He took on enormous financial risk because he had faith in himself and his vision, and boy, was he right! The incredible faith he had in himself and his vision for the original Disney theme park allowed him to take on and overcome tremendous financial risk and avoid unnecessary failure. Multiple movies, theme parks, characters, comics, merchandise, clothing, and toys later, his faith and ability to face seemingly insurmountable odds paid off in a big way. The story of Elon Musk is similar to that of Walt Disney in that his belief in Tesla Motor company allowed him to pony up significant personal assets to bankroll the startup of an electric car company. Both men were large risk takers but had an overwhelming faith in themselves to achieve and eventually saw their vision to completion.

The power of faith is truly amazing when you think about it. Faith has been the catalyst for wars, death, lifelong commitment, charitable giving, and a myriad of other things. If faith can inspire man to such extremes, then surely the faith and belief in yourself can help you ward off risk and prevent unnecessary failures. If you look at someone like J. Paul Getty as a great example of a risk-taker who also believed in himself. The billionaire oil man started small with a $10,000 gift from his dad and turned that into millions by purchasing an oil field in Oklahoma in 1915. If that small gamble wasn't enough, he invested cleverly during the Great Depression at a time when the whole country was hurting. Still out-doing himself further, he then rolled the dice and invested heavily on a desolate tract of land in the Middle East near Saudi Arabia and Kuwait. This was before doing something like that outside the U.S. was unheard of in the oil industry. This gamble in 1953 made him one of the richest men on the planet. While taking risk in your career can prove to be an effective strategy, you may want to consider if that strategy also works in your personal life. Apparently some European kidnappers had not followed Getty's career closely or knew who they were dealing with when they decided to kidnap his grandson back in 1973. The kidnappers initially requested a ludicrous ransom dollar amount for safe return of his grandson but, it wasn't until the kidnappers cut off his grandson's ear and sent it to him via the Italian post office that he decided to stop taking risks with his family member's life. Getty eventually worked a deal to get his grandson back at a far lower price but at what cost? Getty is a good reminder of how we need to balance risk in our professional and personal lives in an effort to avoid unnecessary failures in our life.

Is there a hidden message behind your failure? The fact that you failed at something also means that on some level you tried and that you took on risk. I don't want to be one of those people who says we shouldn't keep score in little league and that everyone gets a trophy, but *trying* is something to be commended. And believe it or not, not everyone tries or makes an attempt at success. Many are content sitting in their comfortable box and doing only what they need to do to keep afloat, nothing more. These people never take risks. So even though something may not have worked out exactly the way you had hoped in the past, you still have done more than a huge majority of the other slobs out there who won't even get up off the couch! Sometimes the best way to learn is through those experiences you've gained where you've fallen flat on your face. I'm not encouraging everyone to go out there and fail on purpose. Quite the opposite. Please be wildly successful. But if you do, in fact, want some success as a leader, you need to step out of your comfort zone and take on some risks. You need to fail. In many cases, it will pay off in the long-term, and if nothing else, it will help you avoid that same pitfall the next time you are in a similar situation.

> You need to fail. In many cases, it will pay off in the long-term, and if nothing else, it will help you avoid that same pitfall the next time you are in a similar situation.

Now back to the key question: how much risk is enough? When I think of leadership and risk, I think of the old risk/reward paradigm. Ever heard of that one? It's the thought that the higher the risk you take, the higher the reward. Most of the time people apply it to stocks and investing, but it also applies to many other things in life, and leadership is one of them. The bigger the reward you seek (leadership, money, freedom, etc.), the higher the risk you should take. So you should think carefully about what you desire and match the amount of risk to meet that goal. I wouldn't suggest you mortgage your house and go gamble it in Las Vegas to try and achieve your goal, that is a nonsensical risk. But you should think about what you want and what you are willing to lose to get it. How big are you willing to fail? Let me say that again, what do you want and what are you willing to lose to get it? The mindset should be that if I want something bad enough, what type of failure am I willing to endure? You must fail to succeed, you just need to decide how big you want the failure to be.

I would bet most of the folks reading this book haven't failed or even taken on any risk in their life. Most of us are wired to be risk averse. You will not succeed at anything if your life is void of risk. If you don't take on any risks, then it is unlikely you will ever fail. It is also very unlikely you will ever succeed. Be sure to take calculated risks in your career, sports, church, investments, and everywhere else. The best outcome you can hope for is a gentle failure. If you've never really failed, go out and plan your failure today. Make sure it lines up with your risk tolerance and then go let it rip. The best leaders and best stories come from failure; don't be boring and bland. Go on and take some risk.

Balancing Act
While we want to fail some of the time to help stretch our boundaries, learn important lessons, and grow as a leader, we certainly don't want

to fail *all* the time. Failing in every facet of your life is not good, but striving to reduce the *unnecessary* failures in your life is also an amiable goal. Provided we can agree that failures are going to happen, it's always a good practice to limit our unnecessary failures by always doing quality work, whether it be at home, church, in the office, the playing field, or beyond. We should all strive to our best with what God has provided us. Unnecessary failures, or those things that can easily be avoided, and we typically look back and say, "Man, that was stupid, why did I do that?!" So how exactly can we avoid these unnecessary failures, these times when we shoot ourselves in the foot? As somewhat of a failure expert myself, having made or been involved in damn near every unnecessary failure you can imagine, I have an opinion on this topic. And it starts with balance...

Details matter. People who naturally are detailed and methodical seem to make fewer silly mistakes, and in many cases, have fewer unnecessary failures. They focus on the little things. They still fail, but they fail *on the good stuff and for the right reasons*. Every time I find myself in a hurry or not properly focusing on the details, my work ends up being done poorly and with mistakes. I see this with my kids and their homework ALL the time! Every time my wife or I sit down with them to go over their homework assignment, we always ask, "Did you check your work?" And of course, every time they say, "Yes, Dad!" with an irritated look on their face. And almost every time I find a simple little detail that they overlooked or missed, causing the entire problem to be wrong. Given that I, too, sometimes struggle to focus on the little things, this happens to me a good bit as well. Don't get me wrong, I am very good at what I do, but I've also learned that I have to force myself to slow down a little as I've gotten older, especially since being detailed is not easy or natural for me. But I've learned from my mistakes when I rushed and sometimes I learned the hard way.

I'll never forget one of my old managers. He was a stickler for the details. We were working on a client proposal one time and he asked me to take a crack at the first draft. I grabbed a prior version of an old proposal and quickly cranked out what I thought was a final product. I was proud of my ability to be efficient and leverage past work to my benefit. I sent the proposal over to him for final review, and after ten minutes, he had sent it back. Like Ralph in the movie *A Christmas Story*, I was certain that my boss would give me glowing remarks (an A++++?) on my work and compliment my genius. However, much to my surprise, he very succinctly asked me to please review it again and to start over. I was stunned. Why would I need to review it again, it was already perfect! But after a quick review, I found multiple stupid errors and mistakes. It was actually kind of embarrassing when I look back on it. What if I had decided to send that directly to the client? It would have been an epic failure and we certainly would have lost the work. This painful lesson taught me to try and slow down in all facets of my life so that I can be positioned for success.

I've also noticed that as I progress in my career those leaders who are successful are typically pretty thorough and don't miss many of the little things. Not trying to draw a direct correlation to success and the details, but it's not an accident that winners often times pay close attention to the little things. They are able to catch those items that the average person might have missed, and that trait has helped them move up the ladder and avoid the unnecessary failures most of us fall into when we are in a hurry or not paying attention. Remember that paying attention to the small things count, and if you still do not believe the little things count, ask the makers of the Hubble telescope.

The Hubble telescope was created to be launched into orbit and allow for high resolution pictures to be taken of outer space that are not inhibited by the Earth's atmosphere. The Hubble Telescope was named after American astronomer Edwin Hubble, who was a pioneer in the field of extragalactic astronomy. The project for the Hubble Telescope was conceived as far back as 1970 and had a total cost in the neighborhood of $1 billion dollars to create the telescope and get that sucker into orbit. NASA spent years constructing the telescope, and getting it into orbit was also not a small undertaking. Once they got the telescope into orbit and the images started coming back, they saw there was a problem. The images of this $1 billion camera were blurry and distorted. Decades of work put into the project with the sole purpose of taking clear pictures of outer space and it wasn't working.

Turns out the primary mirror used for taking the intergalactic pictures was "off" by 2.2 micrometers. A micrometer is a damn small unit of measurement (about 0.000039 of an inch to be exact). However, just like in life, those little details can lead to a big failure. A billion dollars spent on an ineffective telescope equals failure. The silver lining is that they fixed the Hubble telescope since then (a feat that was as miraculous as the construction and the original launch itself), and it has taken some of the most amazing images of the cosmos you can ever imagine. So in the end, they learned from this failure and made a correction they *hopefully* will not repeat. Do a quick search on Hubble telescope images and you'll see what I mean. Amazing.

Details matter, however, I also know people who are so detailed, it is a hindrance to their professional/personal life. Paralysis by analysis is a real thing, and I've seen people that move so slow and deliberately that they can hardly get anything done. An amazing ability to focus could hinder efforts to be productive and successful. In every leadership role, you need to be able to *balance* the details but also look at the big picture. Each person needs to take stock in their own ability to be detailed, good or bad, and determine where they are on the spectrum and how to bridge that gap to success. Sometimes *too* much focus on the details can also lead to unnecessary failure. One such person comes to mind.

I was leading a big system implementation at one of my clients and was working closely with a group of technical architects. One of them, Erika, was unflappable. She was super smart, very composed, and extremely thorough. You could not get her heart rate above 50 beats a minute and she was a perfectionist to the extreme. The struggle I had with Erika is that I knew all of her technical designs and solutions would be flawless, but she took FOREVER to deliver them. She would tirelessly pour over the functional specifications, review it three and four times over, conduct research, and anything else she felt appropriate to deliver a "perfect" final product. While I loved that her designs had such high quality, on one particular project, I was on an incredibly tight budget and timeline. We literally were going to have to push the go-live date, resulting in budget and timeline overruns because we were all waiting on Erika's final designs. It was really tough because I didn't want her to not deliver an excellent final product, but there had to be a balance. She also wasn't so great at delegating, which made things even more difficult. Again, she loved the details! I finally sat down with her and started with the positive message of her excellent final product. I also laid out the challenge I had as the overall project lead in trying to meet a deadline and her work being very behind. We eventually got to a happy medium, but this was a situation where someone's acute focus on details almost cost us!

Equally as important as fine-tuning the details is looking at the big picture. People that are very successful have an uncanny ability to also see the big picture, in addition to the minute details. I have been with some very successful leaders who have had an unbelievable ability to see the larger picture, predict what people will do, and are thus prepared to deal with those situations. They see the big picture of the race and not just the immediate hurdle that is right in front of them. Leaders of any organization are paid to be visionaries and help guide and direct the ship that is their company. How can they do that when they are in the bowels of the ship tinkering with the engines? Making sure the ship is running properly and paying attention to the details is key to saying afloat, but leaders also need to drive and direct, which can only be done when looking out onto the horizon for the next iceberg. I'm sure Captain Edward Smith would have appreciated this analogy.

Captain Smith was the captain of the RMS Titanic, and despite several warnings from other ships, he ran his ship full speed into an iceberg which sank it, killing some 1,500 people (you guys have seen the movie, right?). It was a horrible tragedy and who knows what really happened when the great ship went down, but my gut tells me Captain Smith wasn't looking as closely to the "horizon" as he should have been. Perhaps his flaw was that he was too focused on his pre-planned route and timeline for arrival, which caused him to not look out onto the horizon or ignore warnings from his team. Being able to balance the little things and the big picture will help you navigate through the many potential failures that are out there in your life. Details matter but so does the vision and roadmap. Without balancing both, you will struggle to have any level of success and will learn very little from your failures.

Seeing the big picture and not getting sucked into the "weeds" is sometimes hard. When I was a waiter in college, I remember going through training and hearing the term, "in the weeds." I never truly understood it until my first day on the job. The first day, a Friday, started off easy with just one table who had a simple order with no appetizers, no dessert, and they simply ate their dinner with no fuss or complaints. I thought, "Man, this is easy. I thought everyone said waiting tables was hard." Then came table two and three right on top of each other. Both had complicated orders. Hold the mayo. One wanted fries instead of broccoli. One table ran out of ketchup. Then table four showed up. They were demanding and wanted to order right away, but I had three other requests from my other active tables. Next thing I knew, every time I walked by one of my tables, somebody needed something. In a span of ten minutes, I was completely in the weeds. Now I knew what it meant. Down in the dirt and I couldn't see any way out of it. Surrounded by disgusting, irritating weeds with no blue skies to be seen. I got back to the kitchen and instinctively shouted, "I am in the WEEDS!" This sent a more experienced server over my way, who calmly and slowly asked what was needed, wrote it down on their notepad, and proceeded to seamlessly take on three of my items while still perfectly serving their five open tables. I struggled big time that first day and almost considered walking out...literally. But I hung in there and got through it. At the end of the night, I pulled the more experienced server over to the side and thanked her profusely for helping me out in a pinch. She was very understanding and noted that everyone who has served tables has been there before. I asked her how she did it and she just smiled and laughed. She said different from me, she was able to look at the big picture and not get overwhelmed. Instead of looking at all of the little detailed tasks piling up and getting overwhelmed, she had a system of looking at the list and prioritizing. She knew which items were truly urgent, which items she could delegate to the bar or to the bus boys, and which ones could simply wait. She noted that instead of just blindly running around trying to do everything on the list, she calmly took a breath and applied her strategy. And she did it all with a smile, noting, "Listen, the customers can see when you are stressed and it impacts them in addition to how much they tip you." I had noticed my tips weren't as high as I was previously told. She continued, "If you don't have a plan or way to see the big picture, then everything seems urgent and you'll run yourself ragged trying to do it all. It's not possible." The big picture, I thought. Her words cut like a knife because I clearly had no plan or strategy on what to do. After that first day, I vowed to have a plan for my next shift, and while it was still rough getting through it, it was *way* better than the first. In addition to seeing the big picture, I was getting better at the individual tasks. I even caught myself falling into my old traps and slowed myself down to prioritize and line up my strategy. As leaders, how many times do we get so caught up doing the actual tasks or getting into the weeds that we waste time and energy. Maybe had we looked at the big picture, we would be more efficient and avoid some of those failures unnecessarily encountered along the way.

There was one other time I remember when I got too lost in the details and didn't consider the big picture. I was in fourth grade and had this really awesome teacher, Ms. Jones. She was a great teacher, and sometimes instead of teaching whatever was in the textbook that day, she would go off script and give us *real* learnings. True life lessons. One day we just sat down for math class and she noted that we were going to have a pop quiz. This was really unusual as Ms. Jones was typically very fair and sweet and had never surprised us with a pop quiz or test. Everyone kind of murmured and looked around at each other in confusion. She commented that her class was very bright and that she knew we could successfully ace this exam. I felt a small bead of sweat form on my brow. She handed out the test and it looked something like this:

+++++++

Ms. Jones – 4th Grade Math
Test #5

Name: Jody Dawson
Date: April 4th, 1987

Instructions: Please carefully read *all* questions before starting the test. You have five minutes to complete this test.

1. Which of the following numbers are prime numbers: 12, 7, 16, 24
2. Louisville and Bardstown are 100 miles apart. If train A is leaving from Louisville and headed for Bardstown at 25 miles per hour and train B is leaving Bardstown and heading to Louisville at 10 miles per hour and both leave at the same time, how long before they cross paths.
3. Your favorite aunt is flying to your house next month. She's coming from San Francisco to Buffalo. It's a 5-hour flight and she lives 3,060 miles away from you. How fast does the plane go?
4. On the 12 days of Christmas, how many gifts did the 'True Love' receive? (Partridge in a Pear Tree, 2

Turtle Doves, 3 French Hens, 4 Calling Birds, 5 Golden Rings etc.) How can you show your work?

5. You and two friends are ready to share your birthday cake. Just before you cut the cake, a 4th friend comes to join you. Show and explain what you will do.

6. Your uncle gave you a gift certificate for $50.00. You are going to try to spend every penny! Your choices are: Movie Passes: $12.00, Arcade Passes $14.00, Recreation Passes: $22.00. What will you buy to come as close as possible to spending all of your $50.00?

7. At your skating party, you noticed 30 legs on the outdoor rink. How many people and dogs are on the outdoor rink?

8. Now that you have carefully read *all* of the questions, please only complete question #1 and then put your pencil down and sit quietly.

+++++++

Many of you have probably had a similar test. Like most everyone in my class, I saw that we had five minutes to complete this test and panicked. I easily got the first answer right and then plowed forward to the second, which took forever. I was so hurried and rushed, I didn't notice the two to three students who were sitting there quietly with a smirk on their face as the rest of the class were about to have a nervous breakdown. I barely completed answer #3 when Ms. Jones said "Time." My heart stopped. I had failed this test and failed it badly. She then very sweetly called on one of the clever students who had actually followed the instructions and saw that we were to read all of the questions before answering and #8 instructs you to put down your pencil (some of you maybe even missed this above!). These students had seen the big picture. This test was easy to complete in five minutes, but you had to see the big picture and not get sucked into the details and perfection. This taught me a huge lesson at a young age, that I had to see the big picture always or it might mean failure on the next real test. More than anything, having that *balance* of detail and the big picture is the combination that would allow me to overcome those unnecessary failures on my leadership journey.

Whose Fault is it Anyway?
In some cases, there are multiple people who have a role in any given failure. It doesn't always come down to one person's lapse in judgment or expertise, but a culmination of several little things that can lead to the failure. A leader should look at their role in a failure and try to learn from that mistake to build upon it. What did I do to contribute to this failure? Folks that aren't good leaders are the ones that constantly look for someone else to assign the blame. They self-preserve. Of course, there are situations where a failure can be assigned to a single person, but the true leader owns the circumstances of the failure and helps ensure something like that doesn't happen again vs. finding a person to throw under the bus. Do you take the high road or do you take the low road? Do you own your failures and learn from them, or is it always someone else's fault? My daughter recently got a very poor grade on her science test. Like, really not good. When my wife and I sat her down to discuss it, she was full of excuses.

"My teacher didn't tell me. You, Mom and Dad, didn't tell me I had a test. No one gave me the study guides." And on and on and on. Talk about a big teaching moment. I had to explain to her that the best lesson she can learn from this failure is accountability and to own her grades. She really struggled with the fact that she had a failing grade on this test and there was no one else to blame. Nowhere to run, nowhere to hide. Now a middle schooler, she has realized the importance of owning her results and is rocking the academics and taking care of business (sorry, proud parent moment). In some ways, I would expect a ten-year-old to act this way because they are still learning accountability and ownership. But what about leaders who deflect and blame onto others when things don't work? Do you think any team would want to follow someone who acts this way? Does this mentality describe you? College coaches, the good ones, are notoriously strong at owning their failures. The good ones will deflect the focus away from the 18 and 19-year-old kids that sacrifice so much for the school and the team and place the blame on themselves. This happened in the 2008 NCAA tournament.

In the 2008 NCAA Men's Basketball championship game, the Memphis Tigers had a stranglehold on the game. They were up nine points with around two minutes left in the game and effectively had the championship trophy in their hands. From there, they totally collapsed. They missed free throw after free throw and had major lapses on defense, allowing Kansas to come back and tie the game, sending it to overtime. In overtime, Kansas continued their hot streak, stealing away the title from the Tigers in an instant classic NCAA title game. The bottom line is the players on the court did not hit their free throws or play solid defense. The coach can certainly influence these things, but he will never touch the ball, play a second of the game, or take a shot. Despite his team's collapse, coach John Calipari walked into the press conference and blamed...himself. He noted that he had a young team and that he could have taken measures to prevent the eventual collapse. Called a timeout. Called a better play. Coached them up. Whether you believe that or not, you have to commend him for taking the brunt of the criticism. How will you handle a failure when your team is involved? The great part is when you own your failures, sometime magic can happen. It changes the way you view the failure altogether. To take it even a step further, hidden within your failure could be a major success.

Alexander Fleming, the famous biologist, was working on an experiment trying to grow bacteria in his laboratory. During one of his experiments, he inadvertently left one of his petri dishes out in the open for over a month while away with his family on vacation. When he came back to the lab one month later, he noticed that there was something unusual growing in his petri dishes that he didn't expect. Not only was it not the bacteria growing in the dish, but rather a mold that he didn't expect at all. After careful examination of the petri dish, he found that the mold had actually eradicated the bacteria he was trying to grow. This mold turned out to be penicillin. So he had failed at growing the bacteria, which was the purpose of his experiment, but found something even more interesting in its place! After this discovery and exhaustive study and research with his partners, it was discovered that there were useful applications for penicillin and the rest is history. Good job, Alex.

Ever had a Coca-Cola before? If you're one of the five people in the world that haven't, I'd love to shake your hand. You are missing out! Coke is delicious and brings back great childhood memories with my family back in Kentucky (promise I'm not getting paid by Coca-Cola … yet). The inventor of Coca-Cola, John Pemberton, didn't set out to create or make the groundbreaking popular beverage but wanted to create a medicinal drink to help with headaches and other ailments. As luck would have it, he failed miserably in making a good headache drink but instead stumbled onto what was the beginning of the now global leader of refreshing drinks. The drink that started in rural Georgia has now become a multi-billion-dollar industry and worldwide phenomenon and the rest is history. All because he was committed to the product and owned the final outcome.

Hopefully these examples will help you see your failure in a new light. When you *own* a failure, you are personally vested in the outcome. Instead of just acknowledging the failure, blaming someone else, and walking away, you commit to the positive outcome. This is exactly what John Calipari, Alexander Fleming, and John Pemberton did. Will you do the same with your next failure? But what if you had nothing to do with the failure at all?

When I was a young boy back on the mean streets of Louisville, KY, my dad used to tell me, "You are who you hang out with." He told me that even though it wasn't me doing something stupid, if I was with my friends and one of them was a moron, then people would assume that I, too, was a moron (guilt by association). Unfortunately, I had to learn that lesson the hard way when I was 13-years-old, out with a group of friends on Halloween. I'm not sure if it was because of the full moon or because we were dressed up like zombies hyped up on candy, but this one numbskull in my crew thought that it would be a good idea to vandalize some public property. In typical teenage fashion, this person was immediately busted for doing the vandalism the next day, and during his interrogation, he was asked who was with him. Like a cheap suit, he folded instantly and gave up every one of our names. Thanks, pal! All of his "accomplices" were sent down to talk to the Principal's office, and at the time, I could not understand why I was even in trouble at all. I didn't *do* the stupid thing. But then again, I didn't stop it either. Regardless of my actions or inactions, I was attached at the hip with this crew and their faults were my faults. It was a tough lesson of ownership to learn, but it was something I'll never forget.

As the memory of that painful event slowly faded, the importance of who I associated with became more and more relevant. Luckily, I had a pretty good selection of friends, and those whom I associated with throughout high school and college were upstanding citizens and pretty awesome role models. I thank God every day for the unbelievable people I have in my life and I feel very blessed for many of these folks.

It wasn't until I started managing teams of people at work that the importance of my team really started to hit home. As a young professional, I always worked very hard and did my job as best I could and the quality of my work normally spoke for itself. When I became a manager and suddenly was responsible for a team, I had to transition to a mindset where it wasn't just about my performance but about those on my team. On a particular project, one of my team members did not do their job as expected. The team member did not support and foster the client relationship and the quality of their work was poor. I had done my job, but they had failed at theirs. The two other team members had done their jobs, but the one team member's failure was a critical blow to the project and ultimately our success as a team. Their failure was my failure. As any good leader will tell you, you are only as good as your weakest link and you, as the leader, have to own your team's performance. This is a cliché that is used in team sports a lot, but it rings true in the professional or personal setting as well. If you are a strong parent around disciplining your children and providing consistent feedback, but your spouse is not consistent nor a good example (ahem… me), then you are only as good as your weakest link in your family, and your kids won't get that discipline and consistency that they need from both parents. I am guilty of this by letting my kids off too easy on cleaning their rooms. My wife is strict on this topic and I am sometimes inconsistent. How tricky is that for a kid when you have these differences that you constantly have to navigate. Regardless, true leaders own the outcome of their team, not just themselves.

There is only so much any good leader can control. With the proliferation of social media and the speed at which things occur today, your control over your team is becoming less and less. You need to come to grips with the fact that you simply cannot control everything. In many cases, if you are in a position of leadership, you got there for a reason and it isn't likely because you are so laid back and laissez faire about everything. It's because you can lead and take hold of a team or a situation and make it successful, and that might mean you are a control freak. Admit it. I have. It feels good. Go ahead…admit it. Acceptance is the first step of recovery.

As you become a leader, delegation and trust in your team becomes more and more critical and it is something that I (the control freak) struggle with daily. I have worked hard at it and have become much better about relinquishing control. If this is something you struggle with, I suggest you own it and get comfortable with being uncomfortable. The second thing to do here, and this applies in almost every situation, is to surround yourself with really good people. Whether it be hiring great people or having trustworthy friends or knowledgeable mentors, having solid folks around you who OWN their work makes every link in the chain strong. My old firm had a philosophy around hiring which was that you can teach employees most of the skills needed for the job, but there were three things you had to possess which could not be taught:

- Achievement orientation (basically the desire to succeed)
- Work Ethic
- Ownership

Without any statistical data to back it up, I can tell you that it has proven true across the board, especially around ownership. Those folks that didn't own their work and take pride in it were destined to struggle and likely not be high performers. Owning your failures and your team's failures is not an easy thing to do. It takes toughness and high principles but is an absolutely critical element of overcoming the failures in your life.

Simply Stated

What led to your failures? How did you get here? Have you thought about it? Did you have a plan on whatever it was you were trying to achieve? Was your plan too elaborate? Successful people typically have some sort of a plan. Some more detailed than others, but they typically have something to guide them even if in their head. I do see that often times our failures result from over-thinking what needs to be done. People sometimes forgo the simple straight-forward solution because they think it has to be harder than it really is. In many cases, though, the simplest solutions and approaches are the best pathways to success. The higher the complexity of a solution, the more variables it has, and the easier it is for you to fail. For those academics out there, this is similar to Parkinson's Law. Parkinson's Law is the adage that work expands to fill the time available to complete it. In other words, if you have a month to complete a task, your approach and time to complete it will likely take the whole month. It explains why people procrastinate and why sometimes we can overthink our solutions. If we give ourselves very little time to complete something, then I can promise you the design or solution will be far simpler than if we have a month to complete it. The line between success and failure is a fine one, and it pivots on your ability to come up with a good plan and effectively execute upon that plan. The most complicated plan can be great, but if unable to be executed upon, then it's only worth the paper it's written on. Simplicity wins the day, and without it, can lead to some difficult situations at home, in church, or even in corporate America. Take, for example, the merger of America Online and Time Warner.

It was a massive merger, with AOL acquiring Time Warner for $165+ billion. A lot of very bright people said that it wasn't a good idea...it was a great idea. The merging of the old guard (Time Warner) and new guard (AOL), enabling the antiquated monstrosity of Time Warner to leverage the efficiency and cutting-edge technology and distribution channel of AOL. It was the perfect marriage of yin and yang. Well, on paper, yes, but in reality, not so much.

There was a ton of analysis and due diligence done around the merger of the two large companies and apparently the deal really did seem perfect…on paper. But many believed the ultimate "demise" of the organization centered on the differing corporate cultures. There are countless grad school case studies built around these circumstances, so don't take my outsider's view of the matter as fact, but it seems that perhaps they "overthought" the deal in a big way. The downfall of the combined company resulted in extensive job losses and a large decline in market value for the new organization. Something that could have been so promising where two organizations complemented each other ended up being a total failure (by most accounts) because they didn't look at the simple and obvious things like *culture*. Can people from these two organizations work well together? Will they partner together? Will they build strategic relationships and drive two very strong brands to a higher level as one organization, or will they stay in their silos and not come out? Sadly, for AOL Time Warner, it didn't have a happy ending with thousands of employees and shareholders being adversely impacted.

Getting too cute or elaborate can inhibit your ability to execute, especially with something new or different and can lead to failure. I'm not saying you shouldn't strive toward doing things that are complex but rather be selective on when to be complex. If you are embarking on a new endeavor, where you have limited experience, then keep it very simple. If you want to invest in real estate, for example, then I would not try and buy an apartment complex as your first rental property. Start with something small like a condo or duplex and prove that you can manage it before jumping right into something more sophisticated. On the flip side, if you have lots of experience in a certain endeavor, then being a little more complex is acceptable. It's acceptable because you have learned through years of practice and the little things that would trip up a novice wouldn't even slow you down. Look carefully at your approach and erring on the side of simplicity is probably a solid approach.

I love the KISS principle: *Keep It Simple, Stupid*. Keeping things simple is the best way to achieve success and avoid failure. Some of the greatest ideas are things that were incredibly simple. There are countless ideas that generated wild success like the Slinky, Frisbee, Velcro, Band-Aids, and The Snuggie. The secret to their success beyond their functionality was their simplicity. Something simple that could be used for a practical purpose. Keeping your life simple is a good way to be successful and to limit your failures. Albert Einstein led a simple life as a patent clerk before he developed some of the most ground-breaking ideas in physics ever conceived by man. Keeping your life and endeavors simple is a great way to avoid failure and foster success. Some of the greatest organizations tirelessly pursue simplicity and make it a focal point of their being. Apple has done this for many, if not all, of their products. All designed simply so that even a child can use them. If the things they do are overly complex, then they scrap those ideas or practices. Some of the simplest ideas are the most brilliant. Applying this principle to your endeavors regardless of the magnitude, I am convinced, will yield great results. Keep it simple.

I Doubt It...

So you fail every once in a while, who cares? No big deal, right? Didn't the author of this book just say that everyone fails? So why should I care about failures? Yes, it's true that everyone fails once in a while and that it is part of the human experience, but if not careful, a failure can take on a life of its own. Most of us want some level of success and anytime we fail it hurts. When we are vested in something and it slips away like sand between our fingers, it can be a big hit to our ego. This negative momentum can really hurt our confidence levels, and in some cases, plant a seed of doubt that can become a runaway freight train. Confidence is such a powerful thing regarding your ability to perform, and when you have it, it can be a major catalyst and propel you forward. When you don't have confidence, when you doubt yourself, it can erode your performance, lower self-esteem, and lead to larger issues, like stress, anxiety, and depression. Simply believing you *can* do something takes away most of the other internal, mental distractions and allows you to do your very best. Not believing in your ability to do something makes those voices in your head very loud and obnoxious.

"You can't do that job; you've never done it before."

"Your communication is awful; how could you ever speak in front of a large audience?"

"You really cannot do anything right. What do you have to offer anyone?" Those voices just won't shut up! Failing at something can sometimes bring into question your ability to do that thing or *anything* of substance. The magnitude of the failure can disrupt your confidence in areas where it really doesn't even make sense. I've experienced that first hand.

A few years ago, I tried to start up a new business. I linked up with two other super smart and talented people, and together, we hatched this really cool web-based platform around accelerating volunteerism in the local community. To be fair, one of the other guys was really the brains behind the idea and deserves the credit. The idea was pretty rock solid when first presented to me, and every time we pitched it to someone, we got a similar reaction. "Wow, what a great idea!" But for many different reasons, the business never got off the ground. The platform was slow to take shape. We had no real capital. We struggled to monetize it. We shifted course a few times along the way, each time diminishing the value of the platform. But more than anything, the three of us all had very occupied lives, full-time jobs, and young families. Trying to "fit this in" with everything else going on was very difficult to say the least. We eventually decided to call it quits. Despite encouragement from friends and family we made the tough decision to shut it down, it still felt like a big-time failure and all of us beat ourselves up about it. Because this one hurt so bad, and I felt I had not fully contributed to making it a success, I started to doubt myself in other areas. If I had failed at this endeavor, was I really any good at my current job? Good at being a dad? A husband? Maybe I've been a fraud this whole time and never really delivered anything of substance in my life. Dramatic, I know, but the seed of doubt had been planted and was growing inside me.

When something doesn't work out it, it doesn't mean you are not good or valuable in total. Don't let one setback wash away all of the other good that has been done or diminish your unique talents. You are not the sum of your failures alone but rather the sum of your failures *and* successes…and those aren't black and white. To dig out of this hole, I had to talk about it with my mentor. Talk about it with my wife. My friends. Anyone who would listen. They kept reminding me that even considering doing this outside of my other commitments showed ambition and leadership. They also reminded me to take my own advice and reflect on what else I could learn from this failure. Commitment, practicality, realism were all lessons learned from that failure which I applied to this book, my current job, and my personal life. All have paid off and helped weed out that seed of doubt that was planted. If nothing else, simply getting back to work and the basics is the best antidote for doubt. Hard work wins out every time.

Many of us set goals for ourselves to achieve success. Sometimes we get married to our goals and the attainment of them is all we focus on. For some, that goal-setting mentality can be incredibly powerful and motivating, but if you focus on a specific goal, it can lead you to a place of great satisfaction…or pain and doubt. For me, I was singularly focused on attaining the goal of qualifying for the Boston marathon. At each missed attempt, I would get really down on myself and feel indifferent about the accomplishment of actually successfully completing seven marathons. Instead, because it is something I love, I tried to focus on enjoying the process and setting multiple goals for the same event. I always enjoyed the training, but for the race, I started to set the following goals:

1. Finish the race
2. 10 minutes slower than my personal record
3. Personal record!

Having your goals being multi-dimensional will help remove any doubts around what you can accomplish. Focusing on some of the little things make your over-arching goal more achievable. For example, instead of saying you want to be promoted to partner of your law firm by age 30, you should write down some of the little things that could lead you to that outcome. Goals, like successfully preparing for all your court cases, putting the work in to uncover all the details of each case, networking with colleagues and other partners to understand what it takes to be successful, are all things you can control and will breed the ultimate success you desire. Simply saying you want to be partner by age 30 is certainly specific but not something you can realistically control nor detailed enough to be actionable. Preparing yourself, networking, being focused are all things you can control and will help you avoid those failures along the pathway to success. Being married to a singular goal can drive you to insanity…especially if you achieve it! If you achieve the goal and then then you're done, you will be left with a sense of accomplishment, which will eventually fade. If you don't achieve the goal, you feel a sense of failure because you didn't reach it and then that's it. Think about Olympians. Every Olympian wants to win a gold medal and that is their primary goal – why else would they be there? But even if they achieve that goal in many of the non-major sports, there isn't anything else. I can only imagine how hard of a transition this might be if you have that single goal. It's the same principle around losing weight. I have seen so many people focus on a certain body weight or amount of pounds they want to lose. Once they achieve the weight loss, then they inevitably gain it back because the weight loss was focused on a one-time event vs. trying to lead a healthy lifestyle overall. Focusing on the process will help ensure that the failures you encounter don't slow you down from your overall goal or ruin your psyche. Please, by all means, be goal oriented, but set-up and establish the right type of goals that are pro-cess-focused to help you achieve the right outcomes so that failures won't be devastating to you overall.

I think there are two types of people out there when it comes to success. There are those that *hate to lose* and that hatred of losing is what drives and motivates them to win. Then there are those folks who *love to win*. Wanting to win and sacrificing to feel that rush is what drives and motivates them. The real difference between the two is how they view failure and doubt. I really do think there is a psychological difference between these types of people. Those of us that hate to lose are the ones that think about what losing would mean to us. How would others view us? How would we feel about ourselves if we lost? Failed? How would our teams feel? And so on and so forth. The things that motivate the "hate to lose" crowd come from a place of weakness, negativity, and doubt. We don't want to lose, so we try hard in whatever we do to not feel the pain of losing.

Then there are the "love to win" people. I try every day to be one of these people, and I think I am getting better at it. The type of people who love to win whatever it is that "winning" represents and are laser focused on getting there. Since I am the type of person that truly believes you can change yourself (otherwise I wouldn't have written this book), I also believe you can change yourself from being a *hate to lose person* to a *love to win person*. It's all a matter of figuring out whatever "winning" is to you and focusing in on that. Don't focus on the failure element of the equation – what good can that really do, anyway? Focusing on the success will really change the way you think about things, and more importantly, change your behavior. What do you need to do to win? Who really gives a flip about losing anyway? Focusing on how to win will allow you to overcome any failures on the way to your success. I had a co-worker who always talked about the possibility of getting fired.

"If I don't deliver this project, I'll probably be fired."

"If I don't come under budget, they'll surely let me go."

"It's only a matter of time before they find a reason to rate me poorly and then let me go." And on and on and on... This person was a hate to lose, negative person who spread negative vibes around all those they interacted with. What a bad attitude to have and to express to others. Don't emulate that behavior but instead try to be like Einstein...

No one should win all the time, and if you do, you are likely playing a game, which is not challenging you enough. Push yourself to do more because you may

> If you haven't failed at something, then you haven't tried anything hard

not be unleashing your full capabilities if not properly challenged. If you haven't failed at something, then you haven't tried anything hard. Only when the fabric of your being is stretched can you truly learn and grow. If you don't fail and learn from those failures, you don't evolve. Don't second guess your failures too much – it isn't healthy and plants that seed of doubt that doesn't belong in your garden. Don't take my word for it. Here is what some very wise folks had to say about failure:

> *Far better is it to dare mighty things, to win glorious triumphs, even though checkered by failure...than to rank with those poor spirits who neither enjoy nor suffer much because they live in a gray twilight that knows not victory nor defeat.*
>
> —*Theodore Roosevelt*

> *My great concern is not whether you have failed but whether you are content with your failure.*
>
> —*Abraham Lincoln*

> *It's fine to celebrate success, but it is more important to heed the lessons of failure.*
>
> —*Bill Gates*

> *If you learn from defeat, you haven't really lost.*
>
> —*Zig Ziglar*

> *Remembering that I'll be dead soon is the most important tool I've ever encountered to help me make the big choices in life. Because almost everything - all external expectations, all pride, all fear of embarrassment or failure - these things just fall away in the face of death, leaving only what is truly important.*

— Steve Jobs

In Summary

The winners among us don't treat failures as catastrophic but rather look at them as learning opportunities for us to improve and small speed bumps on our journey toward success. Our "success" in life will be determined, not by our lack of failures, but instead how we deal with those failures as they arise. By taking risk, having balance, and owning your failures, you will not fall victim to failure but rather achieve in the face of the toughest circumstances.

> Our "success" in life will be determined, not by our lack of failures, but instead how we deal with those failures as they arise.

LTF Action Plan

1. Take one big risk per year
2. Try something hard and fail
3. Become a love to win person
4. Be super detailed in one aspect of your life

Chapter 3- Nemesis

Allison was a good person. She had a young family, loved playing tennis with her friends, and her life revolved around running the household while her husband went to work each day (a conscious decision they made together). In an effort to engage and challenge herself beyond the day-to-day of kids, school, and grocery stores, she was an active volunteer at a homeless shelter where she lived. Allison was a very bright and driven person and easily climbed up the ranks at the charitable organization. Besides one other senior, long-time volunteer, she basically ran the show at the shelter. Donations coming in? She handled that with ease. Coordination of supporting the homeless people? She had it covered. Keeping the steady flow of new and one-time volunteers moving through the center? Done. She spent on the upwards of 20+ hours each week at the shelter and had become an integral cog in the larger wheel. Despite the personal satisfaction she got from giving back to the community, things were stressful…and for one reason.

Mark was also a regular volunteer at the shelter. While Allison was sweet and quiet, Mark was loud and direct; Mark was a bully. They always differed on key decisions and were constantly butting heads. When Allison offered up a suggestion or put a new procedure into place, Mark would very openly complain about the change, saying the idea didn't make sense and was not in the best interest of the shelter. He would constantly challenge Allison to her face and demand changes back to the "old way" of doing things. Allison would almost always give in, not feeling comfortable with conflict and justifying it by thinking it was only a volunteer position. She knew her ideas were right but always backed down. The latest battleground topic was regarding a huge new fundraising initiative that Allison was leading for the shelter. She had spent hours drawing up the proposal, working with local companies and supporters to help secure funding to grow the shelter and meet the ever growing needs. Mark did not like this idea. He disliked it so much that he told Allison to her face that it was a bad idea, and when she presented it to the board, he would openly try to stop it.

All of this conflict completely stressed Allison out. She was 100% confident in her approach, knew she had the backing of the board and local companies, and did not understand why someone was so out to get her when they both really had the same goal in mind (long-term success of the shelter). In the weeks leading up to the board meeting, Allison was seriously contemplating resigning altogether. The stress from this one adversary had leaked into her personal life and she couldn't take it anymore. She sat down at the computer, with tears rolling down her face, to write her resignation letter, thinking, "What a shame that one person could derail such an important thing that helps people in need…"

++++

Batman has The Joker. Superman has Lex Luther. God has the Devil and water has oil. Whether you're a superhero or not, everyone can remember a time when they've had a nemesis. Someone that they simply cannot get along with. Maybe this person is a sibling. Maybe they are a co-worker. Perhaps they are someone from college or a rival athlete. Maybe they are even from your church (gasp!). Regardless of the origin, there are times in our lives where we have someone with whom we simply cannot get along.

I am not referring to someone who isn't in your network or circle of friends, people who you really don't know. You can't say the rival college basketball coach is your nemesis because you will really never interact with that person in your life (unless you are, in fact, a college basketball coach). A nemesis is front and center in your face and often the polar opposite of you.

The definition I found of nemesis that I like the most is as follows: *the inescapable agent of someone's or something's downfall*. It just sounds so sinister and awesome and captures the essence of what I am trying to convey. A nemesis is trying to take you down. Okay, that's dramatic, I know, but it definitely helps paint the picture. One of the key attributes of your nemesis is that they are unavoidable.

If it is someone at your place of work or someone in your social circle, then you are going to encounter them. The proximity of this person and your inability to avoid them is in direct correlation with how much of a pain in the neck this person really is. Avoiding someone is never the right answer, but if you don't interact with a person whom you despise, it doesn't consume much of your energy and isn't really a nemesis. On the other hand, if you encounter someone every single day who makes you crazy, then that is a situation you need to deal with.

It's important to distinguish between a nemesis and just having a one-off, difficult run-in with someone. If you work with this person every day for your job, you simply can't not work to avoid the conflict. That isn't a realistic option, and no leader in their right mind is going to tuck their tail between their legs and run away from another person. Any good, sensible leader doesn't wilt at the first sign of conflict or difficulty. Conversely, if this person is in your personal life, then there is some reason that puts you and the nemesis in close proximity to one another. Take, for example, a nemesis I have in my church. Yes, at church! I am very active in the church men's group and interact with a lot of the other committees that do good things in the community. One person that chairs another group and I just don't get along. We clearly have the same values, want to do the same types of things (volunteer, help people, engage in the community) yet, we butt heads. They constantly feel I am trying to take over, do things in a different way, and don't know what I am talking about. It came to a head during a fundraising event where this person openly confronted and chastised me, saying I didn't know what I was doing and was out of control! I have tried speaking with this person openly, one on one, taking different tactics, and everything else you can imagine, but it just isn't going to work. While frustrating, I continue to tell myself that had I not put myself out there to be a leader, do good things in the community and volunteer, I would not have this nemesis. So it isn't all bad. Always keep in mind that despite all of your animosity toward this knucklehead, there typically is some common ground between you both somewhere that will allow you to co-exist amicably.

While the thought of living in a world where everyone gets along may appeal to some pacifists (or hippies), it sounds absolutely terrible to me. Conflict makes the world go 'round. Think about it, without competition or conflict, there would be little progress. Without competition there would not be athletic events and all the great moments they yield. The natural, healthy conflict between men and women is what spawns great relationships and ensures the human race will continue (opposites attract). There is merit in conflict, healthy, reasonable conflict (There is not merit in a toxic relationship where productivity is stifled and you are impacted beyond the individual interaction itself. That stinks…). Having a nemesis who challenges you is a bump in life you will need to deal with at some point in your leadership journey.

Having some element of conflict toward your nemesis can produce two very different results:

1. Growth and development
2. Self-destruction

For those history buffs out there, you may remember an excellent example of a nemesis gone bad….the story of Aaron Burr and Alexander Hamilton.

Aaron Burr and Alexander Hamilton were prominent political figures in the early 1800s and were on opposing sides of the fence, battling for various political seats. Aaron Burr was a Republican and Alexander Hamilton was a Federalist, and they had many run-ins leading up to their fateful duel in 1804. The first of such interactions was in 1791 when Burr won a U.S. Senate seat from Hamilton's father-in-law. Hamilton had been counting on his father-in-law to support his policies while he served as the United States Treasury Secretary, but with Burr winning the New York senate seat, it put a big dent in that plan. Given the close proximity and the constant interaction, they slowly grew into bitter rivals. The rivalry and distaste began to escalate, and in 1800, Burr published an inflammatory document that was very critical of United States President John Adams. John Adams was a Federalist like Hamilton, and that critical document not only widened the gap of distaste between the two political parties, it also created a bigger rift between the two men. For those theatre buffs out there, you can get a view into some of the strife between these two adversaries in the Broadway musical *Hamilton* and how this played out in the 1800 presidential election leading to their fateful demise.

The boiling point happened during the 1804 New York governor's race where Burr was a candidate. Burr decided to turn his back on the Republican party and run as an independent after it became clear Thomas Jefferson would not accept him as the Vice President candidate in the 1804 presidential election. When hearing of this, Hamilton went on an expedition to prevent New York Federalists from supporting the now independent Burr. These two obviously had no qualms about trying to stick it to the other person. Burr ended up losing the governor's race and took on some political baggage in the process. After the governor's race, Hamilton was caught on the record making disparaging remarks against Burr, those of which were eventually published in a New York newspaper and made very public. Having his back firmly against the wall and his future political career in jeopardy (remember he had been a New York Senator and then Vice President), Burr thought the best way to revive his career was through a duel.

A duel in those days was two guys with pistols facing each other with the intent to shoot and kill the other person. Old school cowboy type stuff, which at the time in New York, was technically against the law. Not really the best way, then or now, to settle a conflict. Some accounts suggest that Hamilton wanted no part of this duel, but on July 11th, 1804, there they both stood with a pistol in hand, ready to duel on the shores of New Jersey across from Manhattan and fight to the death. According to eyewitness accounts, each man fired a shot, but it was Hamilton who was mortally wounded and died the following day. Burr was technically still Vice President of the United States at the time of the duel, but his victory quickly led him on a downward spiral with charges of murder being drawn against him. He eventually escaped these charges, but much later in his political career, he hit rock bottom with charges of treason as he tried to remake himself by heading out west for business and political endeavors. Talk about a worst-case scenario. The inability of these two rivals to resolve their issues resulted in their destruction. Both became losers because of it.

Are you currently locked in a battle of wills with someone in your personal or professional life? Think if Hamilton or Burr had backed off just a little bit or tried to extend an olive branch? Then we'd have a different kind of history to reflect upon. Perhaps our history books would tell a very different story. Maybe the history books would tell a story like this.

There are two athletes whose lives and careers are permanently intertwined. From the time they were young teenagers, they competed on the highest levels of basketball's center stage. The two men were starkly different in many ways but similar in others. They both played the game with intensity but one with raw athleticism and incredible gamesmanship, the other with a precise shooting touch and an adept basketball IQ. They frequently competed face-to-face and could not avoid one another as they played in the same league. The competition and the comparisons fueled their rivalry. Both men wanted to beat the other so badly, it raised their games to a level that eventually led each of them to multiple NBA championships and eventually landed each of them in the basketball hall of fame. If you know anything about basketball at all and were born before the year 2000, you probably know I am talking about Magic Johnson and Larry Bird.

Magic, a black man from Lansing, Michigan. Bird, a white man from French Lick, Indiana. Their careers forever joined at the hip because they started at the same time and both had unbridled success at every level. Bird, taking his tiny Indiana State University to the NCCA championship game in 1979, only to lose to the unbelievable Michigan State team led by Magic Johnson. Magic entered the NBA and was an instant success, leading his Lakers to an NBA title in his first year but losing the Rookie of the Year award to Larry Bird. After Magic's huge early success and 1980, 1982, and 1985 NBA championships, Bird could not be outdone and won 1981, 1984, and 1986 NBA championship (Magic ended up winning five NBA championships and Bird won three). The two men were intertwined throughout their careers, and instead of trying to undermine one another, they raised themselves up to the level of competition they faced between each other. Different from Burr and Hamilton, these two men did not tear each other down but rather built each other up and pushed one another to excellence. These two quotes sum up best how their rivalry brought forth the best in each other:

> "When the new schedule would come out each year, I'd grab it and circle the Boston games. To me, it was *The Two* and the other 80."
>
> —Magic Johnson

> "The first thing I would do every morning was look at the box scores to see what Magic did. I didn't care about anything else."
>
> —Larry Bird

How do you want your nemesis experience to unfold – like Burr and Hamilton or like Magic and Bird? Ultimately the answer is up to you, but if you want to master the enemies in your life, you need to accept the following truths that come with each nemesis:

- You need them
- They require change
- Nobody is perfect
- They have impact

These universal truths will bubble to the surface as you continue your leadership journey and deal with difficult people. These difficult people will come and go, but you certainly need them in your life.

You Need an Enemy?

Somebody once told me that you aren't doing your job well unless you've pissed somebody off. Could that be true? I'm not entirely sure, but the way I've interpreted what he said was doing the right thing under any circumstance may cause some friction. Standing up for what you believe ...if you have never had a nemesis in your life, you might be holding yourself back in, despite the naysayers, isn't always popular. Having the courage to push forward on your vision, even when others may not think it is possible and it creates friction.

While I don't condone making enemies, if you have never had a nemesis in your life, you might be holding yourself back. You are not realizing your full potential and certainly not going outside of your comfort zone. We all know someone in our lives who is a jerk, but we also know someone who is the most kind and genuine soul we have ever met. This person wouldn't hurt a fly and they have that down-home tenderness to them that comes from a very genuine place. These people rarely ruffle feathers. In fact, in many cases, you may not even know they are there half the time. We use words to describe these people as gentle, passive, sweet, and sincere. All very fine qualities to have and qualities I would like to see in my team, church, or family but not the only qualities. People like this typically do not have any enemies and seem to lead a simple, stress free life. But they lead a simple life because they are not actively participating in the game of life.

Everyone likes someone who will agree with them, especially when it has something to do with work or a strong ideal they have on a certain topic. People like strength in numbers and having others on their "side" feels good and validating. Those of us who are confident and successful do like to surround ourselves with at least a few people who disagree with us. A healthy dose of challenging assumptions and questioning accepted ideals is how teams and families become strong and successful. Groupthink or a team of "yes men" might be successful, but it means the team is not realizing its full potential.

Think about your personal interactions with your co-workers or family and friends. Have you withheld your thoughts or opinions for the concern of being shot down or not accepted? Of course, everyone has to use their judgment on what to say and when to say it in any situation. You should always apply three important questions when deciding to share something controversial or disruptive:

1. Does this need to be said?
2. Does this need to be said by me?
3. Does this need to be said by me right now?

If you apply the above logic before providing your opinion on something, you can avoid unnecessarily creating an enemy or a fight when one isn't needed. While that is helpful in some circumstances, you should not be afraid to be disruptive. Sometimes things need to be said that are difficult (notice the above questions don't ask whether something is difficult or challenging?). Are you afraid of creating an enemy? You honestly haven't lived until you've stood your ground about something in which you strongly believe in the face of someone who believes the opposite. Even if it hurts someone's feelings. Take, for example, the life of Nelson Mandela.

Mandela was an anti-apartheid leader in South Africa who was convicted and thrown in jail for conspiring to overthrow the government. Although initially a peaceful protester and fighter of apartheid, his move toward establishing the militant *Umkhonto we Sizwe* organization led to the attempted sabotage of the government, which landed him in jail. He was imprisoned for 27 years before being released due to intense racial tension in the country. He stood his ground for what he believed and eventually became President of South Africa, ushering in an era of attempted racial equality which eventually won him the Nobel Peace Prize. While somewhat of a controversial figure, it can't be denied that he stood his ground and was willing to create enemies to rectify what he felt was wrong. If you have coasted through life to this point and not ruffled any feathers, not had some form of enemy, then you are holding back and not living life to its fullest.

If you've never had a nemesis in your life, I'd suggest you aren't experiencing one of life's truly great learning opportunities. You don't really know who you are until you stand up for something you believe in. Don't be afraid to have a nemesis or fight for something in which you believe. In fact, I would encourage you to *practice* fighting by arguing with others. Don't pick a fight with innocent bystanders but argue with friends and family to build up your chops. You should use your your brain and intellect in addition to your fists. Challenge someone to a debate where you have a strong opinion. Argue about politics. Discuss religion. But have an opinion and seek out the conflict in a productive manner and in a way to challenge yourself and others. I would also encourage some physical combat sport or martial arts. Having to physically defend yourself will change your spirit and give you the confidence to be effective in whatever endeavor you seek. Don't believe fighting can be productive in your life? Just ask Bruce Lee…

Most people know Bruce Lee as the dazzling movie star who lit up the big screen with his super-fast and flashy kung fu moves in several blockbuster movies. Most don't know that Bruce got his start in martial arts after getting beat up by some rival gang members in Hong Kong, China. Interestingly enough, his teacher wanted his students, many rival gang members, to spar in his classes so they wouldn't attack and hurt each other on the streets and get themselves in trouble. Bruce parlayed this situation with a rival gang into a mechanism for him to perfect his craft in martial arts and to build confidence. All of this likely playing some role in his eventual stardom and career success before dying tragically at a young age. Some may have read the section above and come to the realization that you have in many ways been sitting on the sidelines displaying little to no fight in any part of your life. It takes a strong character to realize your faults and shortcomings, but more than anything, it takes stronger character to act upon it. Go do something about it! Hopefully some of the insight and shared experiences from above will help you work through these types of situations and be able to do more than just exist with your nemesis but thrive. It's good to fight for what you believe in, but if you look at your life and see that you have lots of enemies, then maybe you need to think about how you conduct yourself. Just like having no enemies is bad, having too many ain't good either.

While never having had a nemesis is a bad thing, having too many is also a problem. You might be going through life half-cocked and not open to others' ideas, or maybe you're just a mean old bully. Regardless, you have the unique ability to ruffle feathers and isolate people, which is not a good quality to have all the time. In many cases, if you are someone like this, you likely sleep very well at night and may even be oblivious to the fact that you are leaving a trail of dead bodies in your path each day. It's this innate ability to either not care or not notice you have too many enemies that is the issue. Congrats to you if blowing people up or making them mad doesn't bother you at all. I sometimes wish I had this ability to not let the well-being of others bother me. Unfortunately, I have the "give-a-damn" gene and care about other people and how my actions impact them. Generally most people are more like me in that they care about others and are not totally insensitive to how their words and actions impact others (some call this emotional intelligence – all of us have it, but the degree to which we have it varies wildly).

I once had a former co-worker whose managerial style was very abrasive and forceful. She was one of those folks that you either loved or hated – there really was no in between with her. She really didn't care what anyone thought about her. This unique style and approach led her to a great level of success, but when she got transferred to head up a different division in the firm, it proved to be a huge downfall. Her style created several enemies, which is the last thing you want to do when going to lead a totally new and separate division within your company.

Sometimes we justify this poor behavior as the right thing to do. Right thing to do for whom? The company? You? Others? When trying to take the moral high-ground to justify your approach, just know that the best leaders arrive at a conclusion and results where all the stakeholders in the situation are winners (Steven Covey calls this a win-win situation in his book 7 *Habits for Highly Effective People*). Most people seek peace and love and will have to push their comfort zone to engage in combat with another person. There is a time to challenge others but it isn't all the time. Make sure you are contemplating this change in your mindset as change is key for dealing with a nemesis...

Times, They are a Changing...
Change is necessary but difficult. It is especially difficult when it comes to trying to change someone else's behavior. Sometimes people have character faults or little nuances that drive us crazy, and we have to deal with these quirks at work, church, sports, or at home. The person that says the word "like" too much. The person that kisses up to the boss in every meeting. The person that walks around with a scowl on their face while volunteering. The person that just cannot seem to coordinate the color of their clothes. These people are not your nemesis, they're just annoying. You simply cannot let others' shortcomings, or more accurately your awareness of their shortcomings, hold you back in any way. The main reason is because changing peoples' *behavior* is difficult to impossible... especially if they are unwilling. You will find that the group of people who are willing to receive feedback, take it to heart, and then change their behavior is incredibly small. If you have someone like this on your team, hang onto to them. Trying to change someone who is unwilling is impossible at best.

I have an aunt who loves to talk politics, and in most cases, we sit on opposite sides of the discussion. No matter how many times I try to steer the conversation in another direction, she brings it right back. It is annoying and it used to make me so mad. Why won't she take the hint? Why is she being stubborn? Why? Why? Why? But I finally realized she was only doing it to rile me up... and it worked every time. I finally looked inward and determined that I took the bait every time she offered. While she shouldn't antagonize a family member, I also shouldn't take the bait and encourage her. On the most recent election,

I promised myself I wouldn't go there with her over the Thanksgiving holiday, and while I mostly kept my word, the level of discussion died down dramatically. Voila! Sometimes in order to enable change in a situation, you have to give in and surrender some control. This can be very difficult for most people but something necessary to change the circumstances you are in. More times than not, small adjustments in *your* attitude or dealings on certain topics with this enemy is the answer. It has been my experience in most cases, modifying my own behavior changes the entire dynamic with the person altogether, just like it did in the situation with my politicking aunt. She hasn't really changed, but I did, and the nemesis situation was gone.

Having a negative force in your life, like an enemy, can be a major distraction. It can almost function in your psyche like a disease would in your physical being. Preparing to interact with this person whom you do not get along with sucks up your brain's bandwidth on a regular basis. And while some people love conflict, most people run away from it. How will I interact with this person when we encounter each other? What will they say to me this time? How will I *change* the situation for the better? Even if you are a confident person, this expected or unexpected interaction causes your sub conscious mind to constantly be in a state of preparation, which takes mental energy away from the present tasks. If you have any productive work that needs to be done, imagine the level of distraction if you have with this ever-present energy and mental drain on you. It is like a parasite on your faculties and prevents you from performing at your best.

Many athletes try to play mind games to throw off their opponents and capture a competitive advantage. In the sports world, there hasn't been many better at psyching people out than Dennis Rodman. Rodman was an eccentric, emotional but very talented journeyman pro basketball player known for his rebounding and stellar defensive skills. He frequently dyed his hair in all sorts of colors and patterns and had many wild tattoos when that wasn't so common in the NBA. He also dressed up like a bride in a wedding dress for a book signing…he's an odd dude. Rodman would typically defend the opposing team's best low post player and was notorious for flopping, pushing, elbowing, and just generally irritating the other player. His goal was to throw them off their game and change their normal performance. He was a true nemesis. He totally disrupted the Seattle Supersonics in the 1996 finals, along with the Utah Jazz in 1997 and 1998 NBA finals, and to countless other teams in the regular season and playoffs. He was a master at getting into people's heads and essentially made a career in getting people to not perform at their best. Your nemesis doesn't have to be a sweaty NBA player with dyed hair and tattoos, but even the smallest enemies can throw you off your game. Know your enemies…

Even the best NBA players in the world couldn't change Dennis Rodman and all his antics and flopping. They also couldn't control the referees or fans. At the end of the day, they can only truly control their own actions and behaviors. They can really only change themselves and control their performance, and the same applies to you when dealing with your enemies. Ultimately it's best if you deal with the situation (nemesis) head on so that you aren't constantly having this mental drag. Dealing with it can happen in a number of ways, but ultimately you need to make a decision on what that will be and then move on. No answer is right. No answer is perfect. But making this decision to change yourself and move forward will allow you to avoid the mental drag and negative energy that comes along with having a nemesis.

The bottom line is you really can't forcibly change another person. You can win their heart through persuasion over time, but forcible change just doesn't work. When dealing with your family or friend who may be a nemesis, a true sign of love is accepting and understanding them for who they are. Trying to change someone simply won't work, and if you do not like the situation, changing your own behavior is really your only shot. Give it a try.

Nobody's Perfect

There is a quote I read a while back that is very applicable to the enemies in our life. "Be kind, for everyone you meet is fighting a battle you know nothing about." I'm not sure the origin of the quote, but it sums up why some people are difficult to be around or work with. All of us have some sort of challenge we are dealing with. All of us. Many may not admit it, but most have some internal struggle they are trying to overcome. I try to do some volunteer work with the homeless where I live and there is a similar dynamic. Volunteers try to ask a homeless person, "What happened?" instead of "Why are you homeless?" Typically, no one really wants to be homeless or a bad person, but something happened to them in their past, which you know nothing about and that thing altered the trajectory of their life.

In many cases, your nemesis may have had some traumatic event that shaped how they interact with others. Can you imagine being the victim of abuse…by your parent? If your trust was rattled by the one person(s) you are supposed to count on most in your life, how might you interact with others you meet for the first time? While an extreme example, this scenario manifests itself in our interactions with others. In many cases, you likely wouldn't despise everything about this person if you got to know them a little better. What if he is a dedicated family man, very active in his church, donates his time to worthwhile charities, enjoys college sports, and likes to run? When I look at this person in their entirety, our value systems are closely aligned. For whatever reason, the nemesis has one personality trait that blocks out the sum of all the other great things this person stands for and believes in. Hmmmm. Maybe they aren't so bad after all? In fact, if this person isn't perfect... maybe I'm not either.

Whether someone has gone through a horrible or traumatic event in their life, we all have faults and opportunities for improvement. Just because someone has one of those faults exposed in the workplace, wagging in your face, doesn't mean it needs to be a huge deal and that you can't appreciate the entire person. In some cases, people with minor character faults are fantastic at what they do but get chastised by organizations because of their minor problems. I have seen this first hand.

Kris was a co-worker of mine who was an engineering whiz. The level of detail and creativity of his designs made him truly one of kind. The products he designed were huge sellers for our organization and literally created a competitive advantage within our industry. He was an asset. The problem with Kris was that he didn't know when to shut his mouth. He had no scruples when it came to knowing what was inappropriate to say and when. He would often times reveal very personal information about himself in a work setting and make everyone *extremely* uncomfortable. He was completely oblivious what he was saying was so awkward, but it would make me crack up laughing! One innocent but embarrassing comment after the other! In addition to this "flaw," he would try to repeatedly start up projects without following the organizational process and chastise people when the project took longer than he expected. All minor infractions I suppose but still... Several people in the organization viewed Kris as their nemesis. Mostly because he was smarter than them and inadvertently rubbed it in their face but also because his weird personal nuances created uncomfortable situations in the workplace. Besides being brilliant, Kris was also coachable. While not a direct report, I would constantly give him coaching and feedback to try to help him. He was open and admitted his interpersonal faults, but I also had to defend him repeatedly to my peers and superiors. Kris was never unprofessional or totally inappropriate and he absolutely got work done, however, his shortcomings limited him from taking his career to the next level.

Just like Kris, you also have personal shortcomings. You have faults. If you don't believe that, then fast forward to the "You" chapter and read carefully. Knowing that you have imperfections should, I hope, make it easier to cut your nemesis some slack and forgive them. We could all use a little bit more grace and forgiveness for our imperfections. Forgiveness of another person takes a load off your back in a major way. Imagine if you were to apply a little forgiveness and humility to your enemy and how that would change the dynamic? Like stated above, you cannot expect your nemesis to change or accept your imperfections, but you can certainly give it a try. What's the worst that can happen?

Perception is Reality

Aside from the very basic human impact, the nemesis can also have an impact in another key area. How you are perceived. People build their perception of you based on your actions in the world and how you treat others. How you treat others, how you conduct your job, your communi-

Your success, or lack thereof, is based on your interactions with other people

cation, your dress and attire, all of these outward things factor into how others perceive you. Your success, or lack thereof, is based on your interactions with other people. Your inability to get along with just one person can make a huge impression on those around you that really matter (i.e. spouse, children, co-workers, boss, etc.). Think about a time when you have seen an interaction where someone was completely rattled by another person. Maybe it was in the grocery store check-out line, perhaps it was in a restaurant when a fellow customer was dealing with bad or slow service, or maybe it was around Christmas time when someone was trying to find a parking spot at the mall (or maybe even church). What did you think of that person? Did you look at that person who was losing their cool in a positive manner? The same is true when we are in a constant state of that "moment of weakness" because of our nemesis. How do you think your boss or spouse or children will view you when you act poorly toward that person? I feel very certain that your outward distaste for this person would not play favorably with your boss, co-workers, or team and it certainly would not play well at home. So in addition to being an emotional drain, your nemesis changes the *perception* others have of you…potentially those that count.

At one of my former jobs, I had a nemesis. For the most part, we outwardly got along with each other, but deep down, we despised each other. She thought I was a moron. I thought she couldn't deliver anything and likely we were both partially right! We were peers in the organization and our boss had set-up a planning meeting for the upcoming year. There was a conversation we were having in between meetings as the group was organizing. We were discussing who was responsible for something, and I felt she was throwing me under the bus. Well, all of that animosity reared its ugly head as I snapped at her in front of everyone. Whoa! In true form, she snapped right back, and suddenly, we had two preschoolers fighting over who was right. It didn't last long, but our boss saw and so did *his* boss. Luckily for me, I had a trusted advisor who pulled me aside later and coached me that it didn't look good. I learned right then that if not careful, this situation could get the best of me and shape people's perception of me that I am a hothead and unprofessional.

In a best case scenario of this situation, both you and your nemesis can come out looking like bozos and the blame is there for you both to share. How bad does the best-case scenario sound? Having that lack of leadership and team work in any sensible organization is going to need to be addressed. Leaders at the company cannot and should not allow that negative type of behavior to continue. It's obvious that the two folks involved have not been able to handle the situation on their own, so what is the next logical step? Likely it will mean that someone more senior in the organization will have to step in and mediate the situation. So, your boss will have to step away from running the business, bringing in sales, negotiating deals with vendors, formulating a marketing strategy, talking to investors, or whatever it is they do and deal with two of his employees who "cannot get along." How happy do you think your boss will be about having to deal with you two?

After mediating between two of his direct reports, what do you think his opinion might be about either of your abilities to handle the next level of responsibility? If you can't handle some lower-level manager, how are you going to handle vendors? Investors? The answer might be that you could handle these parties perfectly well, but after seeing you interacting with a peer and doing so in an unproductive way, it brings in doubt about your capabilities and your long-term potential.

So take the high road, even if it means swallowing your pride. Bad-mouthing your nemesis to other employees or peers, even if you don't do so to your boss, will have the same impact as if you and the person in question simply locked horns on a regular basis. Remember to always keep it classy. It is just as much a reflection on you as it is anything else.

In Summary
Human social interaction is what makes us so unique as human beings and what defines the wonderfulness of living a full and happy life. We

all know that while a big majority of our interactions on a daily basis are enjoyable and within the realm of normal, however, there are some relationships that present unique and difficult challenges for us. While we can all survive through a one-off difficult interaction, it's those interactions that are unpleasant, very close to us, and frequent in nature that pose a challenge. How do we deal with our nemesis in a way that is positive for everyone involved? Just like in most situations, being stubborn on the very important things that matter (morals, principles, etc.) and flexible and open on everything else. But like with everything else, it always starts with you.

LTF Action Plan

1. Start a fight with someone but don't hurt them
2. Change your own behavior with one person
3. Forgive someone who doesn't deserve it
4. Ask how people perceive you at home / work

Chapter 4- Create

Matt was the recent recipient of a promotion at work. Matt worked for a large multi-national industrial manufacturing company as a Vice President of IT. Matt had been with the company for about four years in the same role and was completely thrilled when he got news of the promotion. Finally, he was reporting to an officer of the company and receiving all the perks that come along with that position. More access to strategic company information, direct interaction with the Board of Directors, more coaching and development, and of course, more pay and a substantial annual bonus. He felt this was a great step forward for his family after they had sacrificed for years helping him climb the corporate ladder. Despite this great event in his professional career, something wasn't sitting right with him.

Matt felt that maybe he wasn't totally deserving of this fancy promotion. There had been several internal and external candidates, and at least the internal candidates were all very strong (from what he heard the external candidates as well). Brian, who was currently running the IT Operations group, was a strong technologist and had deep industry and software experience. With his background and current position, he seemed more qualified than Matt. Then there was Margret. Margret had been with the company for 15 years, growing up through the ranks at one of the local plants, eventually moving to headquarters to take on larger roles in Accounting and Finance. She had a true, in-depth understanding of the business processes and knew everyone that mattered on a very personal level. She seemed more qualified than Matt. Finally, there was Al. Al was a hot-shot MBA graduate who was flying up the corporate ladder. Everyone assumed that someday he would be CIO, or possibly even CEO, with his stellar intellect and deep analytical skills. While younger than Matt, Al was clearly the "chosen one" who had been plucked from a top school and was being groomed to take on a big leadership role with the company. The VP of IT role would have made perfect sense for Al to step into with a then clear path to executive leadership in three to five years. When he compared himself to these internal candidates across the major dimensions (communication, analytical skills, experience, and intellect), he felt all candidates scored higher than he did. The only thing Matt could put his finger on that he maybe had over these candidates was creativity.

Matt had come up with an innovative way for the IT team to be more efficient in delivering solutions using automation. So innovative that he published a paper on the topic and spoke at a national industrial manufacturing conference on the benefit to the company. Additionally, through some sharp restructuring work, he also created a new track on his current team, allowing others below him to have a separate career path within the IT group. Matt had also worked diligently to create a fun and trusting culture within his team that fostered great results and collaboration across the various functions (he received an annual internal award for his creativity on team-building).

But even despite some of these "one-off" examples of creativity, his overall set of competencies was no match for the other candidates going for the job. Could this seemingly simple and benign trait of creativity really make the difference in his leadership path? Surely, possessing the basic traits everyone associates with leadership is the main driver in being promoted, right?

++++

We live in a constantly changing world: one that is built on growth and advancement. You might have heard the old adage, "If you're not growing, you're dying" (the quote was attributed to Lou Holtz if I am not mistaken). While a little morbid, the quote underlines the need to adapt when everything around us moves forward, shifts, and changes. To say it in a gentler, humbler way, if we're not moving forward, we are certainly moving backward. While it pays to be nimble and flexible in this real-time and fast-paced world we live in, I think it also calls for something a little different. In my opinion, being flexible and nimble in today's world is simply the price of admission to be a successful leader in the modern-day workforce. Doing that simply gets you in the game but doesn't mean you will win and certainly doesn't mean you will be an effective leader. Just like today, having a bachelor's degree is the bare minimum to even be considered for any decent job. So, what is that little something else that any fledgling leader will have to do in order to take the next step? They have to *create* something.

What does that mean? Is the ability to create something really an inevitable bump in the road of your career or personal life? Think about a famous leader, politician, or business person who runs a large organization. Many times we become mesmerized by these people and their ability to lead, but we can't always define what it is about them that draws us in. Maybe it's because of their position or stature within the organization? Maybe it's because they are effective communicators? Whatever the case, we have to assume they are successful because they are very capable at what they do. But what else got them there? There are so many things that go into the many facets of great leadership, but one thing is fundamental to each leader: they have to be able to create something exceptional that is bigger than themselves.

The definition of *create* is as follows, "cause (something) to happen as a result of one's actions." I've also heard it defined as "bring (something) into existence." I like these definitions, but I think they are void of a key element for our leaders out there, and that is having your creation being larger than yourself. It has to have a multiplier effect and cannot only benefit you. Regardless of how you define it, the inability to *create* is the one bump in life that causes the most of us to get stuck as a leader, and it can be really tough to break through it.

Create exceptional sales. Create an exceptional team. Create an amazing culture. Create growth and scalability within a particular division. Create security or an environment of compliance. Create innovative products and services. Create value for shareholders. Create a sense of hope when the situation might seem dire. Create wins and championships. Creation or creativity is often not something that the traditional leaders think about on a daily basis. Many leaders live in a world of budgets, sales numbers, wins, losses, metrics, and other binary and measurable targets. Creativity is one thing that doesn't thrive in that very black and white world. It's soft. It's fuzzy. It's dirty. It's not always clear and for many leaders; it is very difficult to come to grips with. That is why it matters. Creativity taps into that part of the brain that doesn't always get flexed in our daily life. It ain't easy, but it's so critical! Simply put, if you cannot create, you cannot succeed as a leader.

Think about Abraham Lincoln, the 16th President of the United States and the leader that helped free an enslaved people and guide the nation forward through a crippling Civil War. But what was it that he created? There are more Lincoln historians than you can shake a stick at it, and I'm sure many of them might not agree with me, but I think Lincoln used his amazing communication skills to create consensus and buy-in. He created a vision for the future. He created *hope*.

Think about what he was trying to do in the United States at a time where there was no semblance of human rights or equality for people of color. The very thing he was trying to tear down had huge economic and social ramifications to the people in the southern states. What he was trying to do would have a dramatic impact on their hearts and minds. Needless to say, the odds were not in his favor. Whether it was through his timeless writing skills, his tall and powerful presence, or his ability to deliver the critically important message through speech, Lincoln was able to get a divided nation, government, and constituents to pass the 13th Amendment. He created hope to a people that were treated poorly and had no sense of equality in their life. Hope for a young nation that there was a path forward after the Civil War, even if not everyone believed in the path at that time. Hope that good would win out over evil. Lincoln created hope, and when times are bleak, sometimes hope can be a very powerful thing.

Think about some of the most successful people of our time. Sam Walton. Steve Jobs. Bill Gates. Oprah Winfrey. Henry Ford. These are some of the most successful people to ever walk the planet, and that's because they were able to create something exponentially larger than themselves. These winners created products that changed the way we do things, the way we dress, or even how we get from point A to point B. They were creative and innovative and had revolutionary ideas and products. Let's start with Bill Gates.

Born in Seattle, Washington, Bill Gates was a smart kid who showed lots of academic promise growing up. He scored well on the SAT and landed at the prestigious Harvard University, where he spent one year before dropping out to start his own company. A little company called Microsoft. Most of us know the history of Microsoft's rise to stardom and how its products became the cornerstone of the multi-billion-dollar PC industry. The operating system was the focal point of utilizing personal computers and helped create this industry and change the way we interact in almost every way. So what exactly did Bill Gates create? You could argue that he created a bunch of things. A very successful team and company. Several pieces of amazing technology. Tremendous revenues and profit for shareholders. Countless jobs and career opportunities for people around the world. The financial engine for the Bill and Melinda Gates charitable foundation, which funds countless philanthropic causes across the globe. The list goes on and on. Even more fundamental than that, I think he created something very specific. He created a simple way for the masses to use technology. And that simple creation was the genesis for everything else. Pretty remarkable (Read *Barbarians Led by Bill Gates* by Edstrom and Ellser for an in-depth review of his life and details of Microsoft's success).

Phil Knight was born in Portland, Oregon and interested in sports from the get go. He liked to run and was a very respectable middle-distance runner, eventually landing a spot on his college team, the Oregon Ducks (he ran a personal best 4:10 minute mile – quack, quack). After a reasonable track career at Oregon, he bumped around for a bit before enrolling in Stanford's Business School and eventually obtained his MBA. Through his training at Stanford and with his entrepreneurial spirit, he was able to start-up Blue Ribbon Sports, the precursor to Nike. In addition to creating and growing the multi-billion-dollar shoe and apparel company, Phil Knight also created a tremendous number of other products. He created an entire new industry of sports apparel. He helped create a mechanism for greater athletic performance. He created a new international supply chain. His products elevated several sports figures and personalities to the iconic level. He created an empire in the sporting profession and influenced athletes. He created a global brand. More than any of those other things, he created something functional and fashionable and made it into a manufacturing giant (Read *Shoe Dog: A Memoir by the Creator of NIKE* by Knight for details around the shoe company's rise to the top of the footwear world).

FIRE   WEEL   COMPUTR

Mark Zuckerberg was born in White Plains, New York and excelled in his classes as a young high school student. He eventually ended up at Harvard (like Bill Gates), where he helped create a different medium to connect students called Facemash. Facemash allowed students to play juvenile games amongst themselves, comparing the attractiveness of each other. After lots of shifts and modifications, Mark slowly enhanced the platform and started rolling it out to schools and universities in the format that would eventually become Facebook. Once the snowball started to roll down the mountain, it became bigger and bigger and grew in size and mass. Before long, it was a worldwide phenomenon. What Mark created was a new way to communicate, a new way to gather information, a new way to make friends and be social… and all from the comfort of your home or favorite coffee shop. In some ways, this was the creation of social media and the creation of a new communication medium for young and old to use. There are now over two billion people who are on Facebook. Through Facebook, I've learned news that allowed me to keep in touch with friends far and wide: friends are expecting children, have cancer, have died, and are happy, sad, and everything in between. Mark created something bigger than himself and something that over two billion people have found of great use. Need more examples? The world is littered with great creators (Read *The Facebook Effect* by Kirkpatrick for an inside story of Facebook and how it revolutionized the world).

Henry Ford created an economic way for cars to be manufactured. He created a global brand. He created a way for lots of people to own a car. He created an empire. He created the billionaire lifestyle. He created an automobile revolution. Conrad Hilton created a home away from home for thousands of business travelers, a recognizable brand, and loyalty amongst his patrons. Walt Disney created happiness for families and little children, the "wow" factor when enjoying his movies, products, and parks, childhood memories, excellence in service, and lots and lots and lots of smiles. Vincent Van Gogh created beauty on canvass, a unique style, intrigue and mystique, iconic pieces of art, tragedy, and highly sought after paintings. Ray Kroc created a consistent dining experience and product in his McDonald's restaurants around the world. He created a global franchise, food for people on the go, a new industry, efficiency, and countless philanthropic organizations (like the Ronald McDonald House). So while these are all exceptional examples of iconic figures who have created something so grand that they are written about in the history books, not every person who wants to be a leader has to create at this level Some creative geniuses can be right in your back yard…

Bill Smith was a hard-working dad who started up the men's group at his church. He created a means for men to connect and share things in his community. He created an outlet for men who are struggling with their demons to connect and lift each other up. Suzy Jones created an after school tutoring program for kids in elementary school. She created an open, learning environment for elementary-aged kids. She created something sustainable and encouraging for young people who need help. Neither of these two examples are celebrities, but they, too, created something bigger than themselves. For most of us who aren't billionaires or celebrities, creating something tangible is the key. It can even be something that has been created before. You will find that a big majority of things that exist today are a derivation or a replay of something that already existed! There are very few minds that actually create something from scratch. Something that is pure and new. So you don't have to be innovative like Thomas Edison (who is credited with over 1,000 U.S. patents) but rather be able to find what it is you will create and ground yourself in that creative spark that is bigger than you will ever be by yourself. Your creation might carry on once you are gone (either literally or figuratively) and it should be part of your legacy.

Given that the ability to create is somewhat of an ambiguous leadership challenge, there are four facets to it that once known will help make it clear and guide you on your path to mastery. The four key elements of create are:

- Discovery
- Opportunity
- Action
- How?

Again, while somewhat abstract, the ability to create is a major key to your success as a leader. Creativity also allows you to solve the complex problems that leaders face on a daily basis. The four facets of creation will help you break down this leadership bump and allow you to create something larger than yourself in whatever situation you might be. First, it starts with Discovery…

Discovery of a New World

Do you know what your creative "thing" is? Seriously, do you? It's not an easy thing to know about yourself, and I would say I am just now starting to figure it out (maybe…). Sometimes people get confused with what they are good at vs. what they create, and there is a big difference. For example, someone could be really good at writing computer code, but that in and of itself doesn't really create something bigger than you. I am really good at managing big projects and delivering value to my clients on whatever the initiative might be. Part of the reason I am good at those things is because I create great relationships, trust, and a sense of urgency around execution as part of these efforts. I hope that doesn't sound like bragging, but it's the truth. There are several things I don't create, but trust and strong relationship are two of the things that I do that are bigger than myself and positively impact others. Because of these, I can deliver big results in the construct of a team because people trust me and we work together to drive the right results. There may be other things I create, but those are the things I know for sure, and while I can create them in the construct of my professional life, I can also take that into other places in my life, like my family, church, F3 workout group, or whatever (men, check out www.F3nation.com; women, you can check out www.fianation.com).

The funny thing is that most people don't even know what strengths they possess. If pressed people would come up with something generic but few know the specific, tangible thing that allows them create value in the world. In order to achieve high levels of leadership, you need to hone and sharpen your core strengths. Softening your deficits is also good, but to soar the highest, you need to enhance those things that you naturally do well. When you can't figure out what your creative skill is, there are lots of external resources at your disposal to assist. One of my favorites is the book *Strengths Finder 2.0* by Tom Rath. It's a simple read and has an embedded code and hyperlink to take a detailed survey that zeroes in on your top five strengths. Mine are:

1. Strategic
2. Futuristic
3. Belief
4. Developer
5. Positivity

How can you possibly create any value in this world if you don't have a clue about what you're really good at. Pickup that book and discover what's at the core of you and makes you unique.

What else can you do to determine your hidden creative ability? In my experience just about every person knows what they are good at creating. No one knows you better than you! Take some time to think about it and it should become obvious. If that doesn't work, then you should maybe phone a friend…

George Thorogood, the legendary blues rocker, once famously quipped that he drinks alone. With nobody else. Although technically George isn't drinking alone when you consider his good friends, Johnny Walker, Jack Daniels, and Jimmy Bean (making reference to the namesakes of the famous liquor brands that George loved so much). If you listen to the lyrics of that song, it's actually kind of sad and depressing to think about a man drowning his sorrows all alone with three half empty liquor bottles littered around him. But I think there is an analogy we can make here. While George made the tough decision to drink by himself, you don't have to discover your core strengths by yourself. Creating something that is good and noteworthy is not easy. So why put the burden of having to do that solely on your own shoulders? Why not partner with someone who can help you? And also have them help you discover your creative abilities.

Having a mentor is mandatory to success. We'll unpack this a bit more in a later chapter (You), but make sure you find someone you trust who can help see what value you bring and better understand your skills from a third-person perspective. Having someone to lean on can make this sometimes overwhelming task a little less terrifying. The other interesting part of creation is that most times you have to create something based on what the situation calls for. Our world is not static and it seems to move faster and faster each day. Without having a good mentor at your side, it can make the adjustment and the ability to keep up with that pace daunting and overwhelming. Having someone by your side to help in this creation discovery is hugely powerful and can allow you to create something that is good and not something that is disjointed or stale. I bet George did drink alone on occasion, but I also bet he would have had a lot more fun drinking with his friends, and they probably would have created some more really kick ass songs in the process! Don't make the mistake of trying to shoulder the entire burden on your own.

Make it easier on yourself to create and partner with someone to help take that first step in the process after you've come up with the really good idea. Share the idea with them. Ask for feedback. Talk about it with them and what is good and not good. It will make the next steps easier and help bring your creation to life. Far too many of us try to go it alone when we could have gotten our dreams, ideas, and creations out of our head and into reality had we just had a strong partner to help us make that a reality. The BEST creation is typically formed in partnerships where the parties can play off of each other and accentuate each other's weaknesses. Look no further than Steve

Jobs and Steve Wozniak (Apple), William Proctor and James Gamble (Proctor and Gamble), Henry Wells and William Fargo (Wells Fargo), Orville and Wilbur Wright (Flight), Bill Hewlett and Dave Packard (Hewlett Packard), and many, many more. In short, Discovery should come through self-reflection and with the help of your friends, families, and co-workers. The Discovery piece is difficult but not impossible if you make the time.

Many might not recognize the name Shawn Carter, but millions recognize the name Jay-Z. Before becoming Jay-Z, Shawn grew up in a tough neighborhood in Brooklyn, New York called the Marcy Projects. Shawn bounced around multiple schools during his adolescence and dabbled in the gangster arts of drug dealing and guns. Shawn honed his rapping skills and was eventually "discovered" on a MTV show, which catapulted his career forward. Jay-Z's talent and creativity as a rapper is undeniable, but it's through his art that he discovered another hidden talent as an entrepreneur and producer. This creative spark discovered later in his life helped catapult him even further sponsoring and promoting other young artists, along with starting up several business ventures many proving to be very successful. Jay-Z helped create an empire in the music business by discovering one of his creative talents that perhaps he didn't know he possessed when he first started out. What hidden creative talents lie within you that need to be resurrected and developed? Take a look, you might be surprised in what you see...

Opportunity Knocks
Another important question to ask is whether your current situation allows you to utilize your newly found creative abilities? If you have the ability to create great relationships and build trust with other people, but are an accounting clerk, your job may not allow you to share your creative talent and put you in a situation where you are

maximizing your potential. You'll know if you are in this type of situation where your creative spark doesn't fit with your environment if you are constantly feeling unsatisfied or continue to get passed over for promotions. Of course there can be a whole host of reasons why you might not be happy (co-workers, work environment, weather, etc.) or are getting passed over for promotions (bad leadership, poor performance, etc.), but if everything else with your profession is mostly good, but you just feel stuck and unhappy, you likely have a mismatch with your skills and what your current position offers in terms of opportunities. As mentioned before, my three criteria for taking on a leadership position are I like the type of work, I like and enjoy the people I work with, and I have *opportunity* for growth and to excel. Opportunity is the really tough one and it doesn't always mean a better title, more money, or a promotion. It's the opportunity to leverage your God given skills and talents to create. If you feel that you don't have opportunities to shine, don't be discouraged by this; many people have faced this situation…like Bill Belichick.

Bill Belichick was head coach of the Cleveland Browns for five years, amassing a 36-44 record. He only went to the playoffs one time while at Cleveland and essentially was a failure as a head coach in the NFL. As the Browns leadership decided to move the franchise to Baltimore, coach Belichick was let go as head coach. After bouncing around with a few teams, he eventually was offered the head coach and general manager job for the New England Patriots. For whatever reason, the situation Bill had in Cleveland did not allow him to create success on the field. His opportunity there was not conducive to success for him (or Browns fans may argue…for anyone!). For whatever reason, be it control, organization structure, culture, climate, stage of life, or whatever it might have been, Bill was able to create a winning team on the field for over two decades now in New England. He was able to create a *dynasty*. Dynasty includes multiple generations of fans, players, trophies, memories, and on the field success. Now THAT is creating something bigger than yourself. Not an easy fete, and in my opinion, directly correlated with his ability create a winning formula within that organization. So once you have discovered your innate ability to create something unique and you have the opportunity to leverage that skillset, then there is only one thing left to do…

Good ideas and creativity are hugely critical to success as a leader. If they weren't, then there would be a user manual and it would be handed out at every business school, military base, gym, football field, dinner table, or anywhere else leaders are needed. There is no blue-print for being able to be creative, adapt, and leverage your talent and skills to create something unique. If you are unable to create or be creative as a leader, you will fail. Fail. It sounds extreme, but it is true. Each leadership role presents new opportunities to create almost every day. That's why creativity matters and the ability to create is so instrumental to any successful leader.

One great example of a creative leader is Napoleon Bonaparte. Napoleon was the French military general and politician who led France during the latter part of the French Revolution. Many know him as a ruthless military general who ran his armies across most of Europe, Africa, and every place in between. Napoleon is one of those once in a lifetime leaders who people remember and study because of the unique impression he left on the world. One thing people might not think about Napoleon was that he was creative; his creativity on the battlefield won him many battles and great acclaim. As a leader of his French armies, Napoleon was always trying new techniques to win battles as those opportunities presented themselves. He often per-plexed his enemies with unorthodox military strategies. His enemies wouldn't know what to do to combat his maneuvers and formations because they were not seen before or unexpected. He would fight at odd times of the day, fight on consecutive days, fight in the snow, rain, sun, night, or whenever he believed he could get an advantage over his combatants. He looked at every possible scenario as an *opportunity* to flex his creative skill. One such example of this creativity was during the Battle of the Pyramids in Egypt in 1798. Yes, Napoleon fought the Egyptians.

In Egypt, Napoleon faced an army of fearless and efficient Islamic killers known as the Mamluks. Napoleon was significantly outmanned in this battle, but he employed a creative approach in having his soldiers line up in a big, hollow, square formation with the artillery and supplies in the center. His army then proceeded to rotate as the Mamluks attacked. This enabled his army to push them back with a high level of efficiency and then rotate in fresh soldiers. As expected Napoleon won this and many other battles by employing this creative flair in his approach to fighting. He could have very easily lined up in the traditional manner against his foes with a very different outcome for his armies. With the odds against him, had he taken a more traditional tact in executing his attacks, he may have only lasted a few weeks or won half as many battles as he did in real life. Napoleon was an innovator and his creative strategies won him many battles, political power, and a bloody, yet solid place in the history books.

Great leaders can create success for those around them. These leaders can create new sales, new jobs, a positive working environment, learning, education, career advancement, wins, and everything in between. When you are able to create something, you are needed and every organization, team or family needs that creative leadership. That is why creativity and the ability to create something bigger than yourself is so critical. In my opinion, you can only be so effective as a leader if you are unable to create. So while it can be the fuel for your success, it can also fuel your failure as well. Creativity is huge!

Have you ever worked with someone who is stuck in his/her job or organization? Someone who has talent, is a good person, does their job well but just can't break through to the next level or be put in a leadership position? In many cases, this is because the person is unable to create that one thing that is larger than they are. Is that person you? Are you stuck but have the abilities and talent to be a successful leader? Maybe it's because you are not creating opportunities.

If you think creativity is not a critical skill you need to develop, then you are wrong. Most people's jobs are centered around executing someone else's creation. Think about that for a minute. Are you creating your own thing, or are you executing upon someone else's? Typically the top leaders in any organization are creating something for the entirety of the organization. It's an application of the Pareto principle, where 80% of the effects come from 20% of the causes. The Pareto principle was meant to apply to income and wealth among the masses but has applications elsewhere. It's not that 80% of the people don't work hard or try to succeed; it's just that they don't know how to or want to create something bigger than themselves. You may have a creative block and that can put a major stoppage on your career or opportunity for success as a leader. So why should creativity matter to you?

The last and most important reason why your ability to create opportunities matters to a leader is because that unique thing that you create is what makes you *irreplaceable*. It is undeniably you. Fred, who works in construction, creates an amazing culture and environment for his team. Linda, who is a team leader at a bank, creates amazing business development opportunities. Sue, who is a manager at a group counseling practice, creates deep and lasting relationships. Those creations can be undeniably you, and if you were gone, the organization would suddenly have a huge void without you there. Now we can maybe debate about whether your creation should be able to sustain itself when you're gone, but you were the genesis of it and that makes you special and an asset to the team. Your creation has huge value and you should never underestimate its value to your career and any organization that you work for. Now do you see why it is so important to create?

Action Figure

If you know your creativity talent and have opportunities to use it but still aren't getting the results you want, you may need to ask yourself if you are putting your creative abilities into action. Action is the fuel that makes creativity go. How many times have you been at a party or social gathering where some dude has this great idea that is hugely creative? Everyone raise their glass to "Bill," the smart guy with the cool idea. But Bill's great idea is forgotten when you wake up the next day, hung-over, and everyone goes about their business with the great idea a distant memory. I am sure we have all seen the Bill's in our life who seem to be smart, creative people with good talent and opportunities that just doesn't get applied.

I always laugh when people have this great idea for a new business or product but are afraid to share it because someone might steal it. NO ONE is going to take your idea they hear about at some party and go try to make it happen. No one. In fact, most people will give you their feedback, whether you want it or not, which can help shape your creative idea (If someone was

> Creativity without action is just dreaming...and no one ever gets anything done when they are asleep

so motivated to go make your creation a reality, they would have already done so with their own big creative idea because they had taken ACTION). Don't be bashful about sharing your creativity. Put it into action. It's pretty sad when you think about good ideas or abilities withering away. Creativity without action is just dreaming…and no one ever gets anything done when they are asleep. Everyone can dream, but putting something into action is what separates the men from the boys. Creativity doesn't live inside your head but rather only exists when available for all to consume. Dream + Action = Creativity.

Action! Lots and lots of people have come up with great ideas that never turned into anything. Ideas like fuel cells, new Coke, XFL, DeLorean cars, Betamax movies, and a whole host of other creative ideas that never really took off. Most of us come up with good ideas to implement in our place of work or at home, yet we are too lazy or not confident enough in ourselves to even try. It's crazy, right? So why don't we take action? I believe the thought of trying to bring our idea to life seems so big that it paralyzes us from taking action. Whether it's fear or laziness, taking the first step is the hardest. I know for me once I can take the first steps on anything, the subsequent steps are much easier to take. So to combat the lack of action, just take one step. *One* step. That's it. Taking one step will no doubt trigger the next and the next step, but it's the first one you have to take that is the most difficult. A great example is the finalization of this book. I always struggled to find time to complete the final editing and close out the comments from my editor. I did find that if I never took out my laptop or opened the document, then I never got anything done. As soon as I would get my laptop out and open the document, I normally got sucked in. The initial step and pending time commitment seemed overwhelming and prevented me from starting. As soon as I took that first step, then I was all-in. The dirty little secret here is that the creation is nothing until you take the first step. Your innovation doesn't exist in your head. It has to have air and see the light of day and it only does that if you take action on it and make it a reality.

It took me a LONG time to get this book up off the ground. I learned a lot of things when writing this book but mostly that writing is very tough and takes high levels of perseverance and focus. It takes incredible levels of action. It wasn't until I realized this that I started to make time to sit down and actually start to pound out words in my head. Action. I readily admit that had I spent less time dreaming about what I would write and how I would feel when the book was done and more time sitting at the keyboard, I would have finished this project years ago. But the reality is that it took me a while to put my dreams into action, and I think a big part of that was getting pissed at the fact that it wasn't becoming a reality.

I started small with the outline of the book and slowly chiseled away at the words on the page. Chapter by chapter. Word by word. Dreaming doesn't bring things to life – action does. But you can't have these great things without some level of dreaming. I am by no means saying don't dream big. Quite the opposite. I am saying dream often and dream big, but put that creativity into action before it becomes a distant memory. Put your dreams into action and make your creativity available for those around you to consume. It will unlock the leader within you.

Taking *action* to create something larger than yourself makes you use a part of your brain that is not often used in the normal course of a regular day. Being creative seems very simple and straight forward but hard to do for many. Little kids can create a huge colorful picture in one sitting, so why would it be hard for me to create something, even small, of value on my level? Well, it is actually really hard and not everyone can take the action to do it. For some reason, we are born as little creators and can crank out cool and colorful pictures, make up games, build sandcastles, and create imaginary characters. But something changes during adolescence that makes creation not cool or interesting. Maybe it's because there is such a focus on left brain stuff in school, like math and science, that we just don't work out those creative muscles enough for them to develop. Bottom line – it ain't easy. Because it is hard to do, there may be the opportunity to create at someone else's expense. Creation is meant to be positive and collaborative, and creating from a place of negativity, will only end up hurting you in the long run. The same way that negative or narrow creation excludes others, it will hinder your ability to lead. Our creations are meant for everyone (ask an artist and they'll tell you that), but most artists will tell you that their creations should not be offensive. Offensive and exclusionary creations, while creative, will not be productive or help you advance. If you need an example of where creation was done at someone's expense, look no further than the invention of the radio and Nikola Tesla.

But wait, didn't Guglielmo Marconi invent the radio? Wasn't he the guy that won the first U.S. patent and transformed the way we live and communicate? Technically yes and no. While Marconi was originally awarded the U.S. patent for the invention in 1904, it was actually Nikola Tesla who was doing pioneering work in this field years before Marconi, and *he* actually received a patent for transmitting messages over long distances, leveraging his "Tesla coils" in 1900. Marconi had conducted numerous attempts to get his various radio transmission patents through with limited success and only started to achieve some breakthroughs with his inventions *after* he started to leverage some of Tesla's existing technologies that were developed years earlier (the Tesla Oscillator is one such invention he supposedly leveraged). You can imagine the outrage of Tesla, who had done all this work years before Marconi, achieved success in this field, and then Marconi "leveraged" his technologies and he gets awarded the actual patent. The silver lining is that in 1943, Tesla was retroactively awarded some of the landmark patents (there were several) for the actual invention of the radio. In reality both men, along with a few others, should have the rights to this creation, yet many history books omit this technicality in the inventive process. Be creative but not at the expense of others.

In life there will always be challenges along the way, especially for those things you are trying to create and bring to life. In bringing any idea to life, there is always going to be something that comes up that frustrates you, slows you down, irritates you, and just plain drives you nuts. But that is life and anything good is worth taking action to bring to life. Don't let the fear of failure or difficulty of taking the initial first step. All of us can create something wonderful, but we just have to act and take that first painful step.

How Did You Do That?

Who are some of the creative geniuses you can think of? Steve Jobs? Bill Gates? Mozart? DaVinci? Why do we consider them creative geniuses? Mostly it has to do with their massive success, but in many cases, it has to do with their creativity and ability to create. Genius is defined as "exceptional intellectual or creative power." If we could ask them what is the reason behind their success, they would give a myriad of reasons. Anytime you are able to create something large and impactful, everyone wants to know "how did you do that?"

If someone is rich, the first question everyone asks is, "How did you become rich?"

"How did you start that company?"

"How did you make that sale?"

"How did you make the time to do that?"

If a musician writes the latest hit song, people always want to know, "How did you come up with such great music and lyrics?" People are enamored with the "how" and want to try and recreate someone's special formula for their own benefit. The one thing you won't get from this book is *how* to be creative or be a great leader. In my view, that really only works if it comes from within. But don't take my word for it. Ask Albert Einstein…

Albert Einstein came up with the theory of relativity, which somehow explains the universe. $E= MC^2$. Einstein was a genius, a once in a lifetime "Brainiac." But *how* did he do it? Because the concept of how the universe was formed is so big and untenable, most of us don't really care how he did it. Some speculate that his job as a patent clerk allowed him to free his mind for extensive creativity and deep thought. Others attribute his breakthroughs to some very deep transcendental meditation that freed his subconscious mind to concoct these seemingly impossible equations. One of Einstein's best quotes summarizes it all "I have no special talents. I am only passionately curious". Whatever his *how* was, he took the journey and discovered it for himself through passion and curiosity (action). The dirty little secret here is that *you* have to come up with your own way, and you likely have the answer right now inside of you.

People think you have to look outwardly or somewhere else to find the answer to your creation. They think they do not know how to create, but they absolutely have this ability hardwired in their brain and just don't know how to tap into it. Almost always the person can solve their problem and create something amazing if they just stop and think for a bit. To take it even one step further, I have seen that when I am at my most creative, or when I can solve problems the best is when I am not working, or even actively thinking about what it is I am trying to create. How is that possible? Well, your subconscious mind makes it possible. Your subconscious mind is used for some truly amazing things and is the part of your mind that is lurking in the background. It is the portion of your brain that is working behind the scenes and is the instinctual, powerful part of your brain that can do amazing things, even while you are asleep. Most of us do not use this part of our brain other than for the very core things it does regarding our lives (instincts, desires, fears, etc.). What this part of our mind can do is amazing, if we only unleash it. The best part is that we simply need to present this part of our brain with a problem or creative need and then let it go to work. Unleash your subconscious mind on the task, and before you know it, the subconscious brain is at work, trying to solve the problem or creative idea. The key is that this ally in your head will relay the solution back to you, but you just need to be open to and listening for its answer. Many times it is hard to hear, and you don't notice the answer to your puzzle unless you are truly listening.

Sometimes we trick ourselves into thinking that the more we use our active or conscious brain to problem-solve, the more it gets in the way of the real "brains" of the operation, the subconscious mind. I have used the subconscious brain many times in writing this book and every time it has provided me fantastic insights and thoughts that I had all along, I just had to listen. I normally would get stuck on a topic or not feel a certain part was clear and concise. I would normally write it down as something I needed to resolve. I would focus on the issue for a bit and then consciously walk away from it. I would take a shower. Go for a drive. Take a run. Anything to distract my mind. Literally every time I would distract myself, the result would come in some revelation that I had all along. It's amazing. Don't believe me? Think about a time when you've had a problem at home or work, and then like a flash of light, it just hits you. Bang! The solution is right there, and you weren't event actively thinking about it.

Maybe Albert Einstein was no smarter than you or I, and he was just a better listener to his *whole* brain. This might sound like some Jedi mind trickery, but it really works. If you fall into the category of non-believer around the subconscious mind and that it can really work for you, then think about it this way: You are a smart and capable person who can solve most any problem, dilemma, or creative issue. The problem is you need to relax and let the answers come to you. The best way to do this is to loosen the grip on the issue, step away, and let the answer come back to you once you have cleared your head. Even Buddha himself supposedly meditated and had quiet reflection for days before he received total enlightenment.

In today's world, we spend such little time in reflection or deep thought with all the distractions around us, it is good to have some time to simply think and slow down your mind so it can do its thing. You think it's any coincidence that some of the greatest thinkers of our time imagined some of the biggest ideas and principles of all time when life was simpler and slower? The Greek philosophers, Isaac Newton, Shakespeare, Mozart, Thomas Edison, Sigmund Freud, lived in simpler times where thought and quiet time was valued. Use the same ideas to unleash your best by slowing down and using your subconscious mind to help solve your creative issues. Writer Ann Patchett does not have a cell phone or internet to help her concentrate and focus. I suggest turning off your phone, computer, or whatever it might be distracting you. The beauty of the information age is our immediate and readily available access to information. The problem is that we are constantly bombarding our brain with superfluous information. In order for it to work on what we really need it to, we sometimes have to limit what we are taking in. Ultimately, the how must come from within...

Whether you like it or not, everyone is going to be known for creating something. *Everyone* will be known for creating one of these three things:

- Something good
- Something bad
- Nothing at all

Really only one of those is good and you have a choice over which one you create. In life we don't always have choices, so it's good that for something so critical to our leadership success, we can actually choose which route to take. The challenge is choosing the right path and knowing when you might be headed down the bad path (creating nothing or creating something bad). No one can definitively tell you "how" to go down the path, but I tend to rely on my confidants and friends to help keep me on the straight and narrow. I constantly ask my wife, boss, friends for feedback. How has my performance been (directed to my boss)? Have I been engaged and positive at home (directed to my wife)? Am I on the right spiritual path (to my pastor)? It's hard to tell where you are in the creation spectrum as you are not constantly looking at yourself or your behavior the way others do. How can you know if you are not creating something good if you don't look or ask?

Being positive also helps create something good. Having a bad attitude is inherently going to set you up for doing nothing or something bad. Controlling your attitude and being positive as much as possible is a fantastic accelerator for good creation. I was griping to a mentor recently about the lack of "good culture" on our team and how we really needed to create an awesome environment for our people so they could get the most out of their experience while at work. This leader very nicely pointed out that while I wasn't creating something bad in this area, I wasn't creating anything at all.

She said, "Why don't *you* help make the environment a better and more engaging place, instead of complaining about it?" Dang. She got me there. So it was time to take matters into my own hands and create the culture that I wanted and the experience that I was hoping for instead of waiting for someone else to do it. I griped about how the team never got together outside of work. I decided to do this for my team. I complained that our leader wasn't giving feedback real-time. I implemented this on my team right away. All the things I complained about, I decided to own and fix where I could, based on my personal influence and role. So taking matters into my hands and creating that positive working environment, I was moving myself away from the nothing and into the something good.

It was very hard for me to realize that while I was doing nothing, my complaining about it to a peer was almost bordering on me doing something *bad*. Think about the things you are creating in your world today. Are they all good? How many of them are bad? What about those areas where you are creating nothing? In most people's lives, you probably have a little bit of all of these if you're honest with yourself. The key is to have your friends and confidants help you identify when you're creating nothing or something bad. It is also important to make sure you recognize your team or family when they are creating something that's good. Most of us want to create something good, and when we do and it's recognized, it is hugely uplifting.

In Summary
Creation is a huge part of your personal development as a leader and a big mile marker on your road to success, both in your personal and professional life. One of the truths is that we will all create something in our life, whether we like it or not, and whether we create something good or bad is entirely up to us. Creating something positive in your life will help accelerate your trajectory to being a better leader and help influence others and make you known for creating something larger than yourself. Creating something at the expense of another person will simply deteriorate your ability to be effective and will ultimately bring forward an experience that isn't good for anyone. Leveraging someone else to help you be creative is a sure-fire way to make sure you see beyond the actual creative thought and put it into action. Creating is one of the more difficult bumps on your road to being a successful leader but one that you can master if applied correctly.

LTF Action Plan

1. Write down your creative strength
2. Take one step forward on something hard
3. Clear your mind to solve a creative problem
4. Create one new thing this year

Chapter 5 - Crisis

Katie was the CEO of a large pet food company. The company created the most popular brand of dog and cat food around and was carried in every major pet food store across the United States. Katie joined the company as CEO ten years ago after rising up the ranks in a different industry. The board of directors selected Katie to run the company after an exhaustive search, as they needed a dynamic leader who thought differently as the company seemed to be stuck in neutral. With little to no experience in the industry, the board's choice proved very wise as Katie led the company for 10+ years of great success and growth. Over ten years under Katie's reign, the company took away 15% market share from the then top brand, eclipsed over $1 billion in annual revenues, and started to break into new international markets. Things could not have been going better until one Thursday afternoon, the news hit.

USA Pet Food products were making dogs and cats gravely ill. A contamination in one of their manufacturing plants in South America had permeated most of their products. The worst part is that the quality control *measures at the plant did not catch the issue and word leaked out quickly as pets kept showing up in vet offices with a clear tie back to the pet food. Now Katie was faced with some really tough decisions. Should she issue a recall? What about a press release? How would this impact revenues? Would employees leave over the embarrassment? Despite her great success across her career, she was faced with something she had not encountered before. For the first time…she felt helpless.*

++++

Many of us can think of a time in our lives when something went wrong that seemed… catastrophic. I'll never forget when the stock market crashed on October 19th, 1987. They called it "Black Monday." I remember with great detail how my teachers at school talked about it, noting the magnitude of it, and how they seemed very rattled by the whole situation. It didn't stop at school. My parents perpetuated the bad vibes at home with their nervous looks and whispered conversation. The one-time event seemed dramatic based on the news coverage, but the effect of it seemed to go on forever. I remembered seeing TV footage of guys on a trading floor who seemed to be in shock, freaking out and yelling at each other. What in the world these people actually did was completely foreign to me at ten-years-old. I had no idea what all the drama was about: my dad still had a job, we still had food on the table and a roof over our head. So why was there this negative mood that seemed to go on incessantly as we waited for things to get back to the way they were? It was and still is a vivid and very negative memory, even though I wasn't that old when it happened.

Still another time I had a close family member who was diagnosed with a serious form of cancer at the age of two. He was very young and the prognosis was not very good. I remember feeling scared and helpless, like there was nothing I could really do to help. We visited him in the hospital and he look weakened and feeble from all the medicine he was taking. He looked scared, drained, and exhausted all at the same time. The way the adults acted around me also confirmed this wasn't an insignificant thing which drove my feelings of complete unease and fear in this life or death situation. The whole family rallied around each other and helped make the best of a very trying situation. I remember watching how the adults banded together during that crisis and how to act when things got tough.

Whether on a larger scale, like in the stock market crash, or in a more personal way, like a family member getting sick, it's impossible to avoid crisis in your life. Most of the time, everything turns out just fine and the crisis is overcome, but in the midst of it, there seems to be no end in sight and a huge cloud of doubt looms large. Just the word crisis creates negative emotions within us. Most people do not look back fondly on a crisis and do not want to relive those difficult moments. Most people look back at those critical times and are happy that they are over. In many ways, the people around you during the crisis define the event and whether it is remembered as a positive or negative experience for all those involved. The people make the crisis what it is…

Merriam-Webster defines crisis as "an unstable or crucial time or state of affairs in which a decisive change is impending; *especially* one with the distinct possibility of a highly undesirable outcome." My definition, which I came up with *before* looking at Webster's version (I promise) goes something like this, "A one-time event that usually has both emotional and physical impact to the parties and requires a decision or decisiveness." Ironically enough, old Mr. Webster and I were not too terribly far apart. Great minds think alike. Let's explore my definition a bit.

A crisis has to be a one-time event. Unless your life is the storyline for a romantic comedy television show, then you should not be living from one crisis to the next. We all have ups and downs, but your entire life should not be a crisis. If your life feels like a 24x7 crisis, then I suggest you seek some professional help, take hold of your life, and get better friends. Life is too short to go through it miserable and in "crisis mode" all the time. A crisis will also have both emotional and physical impacts to the those involved. The impact of the stock market crash had an emotional effect on me in that it made me worried about our financial security and safety. On the flip side of the coin, it had a real, tangible impact as it dropped the value of my parent's investments and retirement accounts and impacted the wider economy. A crisis doesn't necessarily need to have both an emotional and physical aspect to it, but when it does, that's when you know it's a real crisis. It has to sting. It has to matter, otherwise it isn't a crisis…it's just an everyday normal thing. Lastly, the crisis requires some form of a decision by the impacted parties. After the stock market crash, my parents decided to move their investments to real estate, which was less susceptible to volatile swings in value. When our family member got sick, the parents decided to get him the proper medical attention and take him to the best care possible. It's really this single decision point that will define how you personally, along with the people around you, overcome and remember this event.

Being able to identify a true crisis and responding appropriately is the hallmark of a good leader. You know you may have a crisis on your hand when you feel an unnatural amount of stress and lack of clarity around the outcome of an event. It's this unknown element that causes us the most angst. Those things, which we cannot control, give us heartburn.

To overcome a crisis, you need to have four characteristics. These characteristics will help you identify the crisis and chisel your way through it with poise and integrity. While some people are born with these traits, others of us need to adopt and learn them over time. They are all attainable and can be developed over time by you, the leader in this situation. The characteristics are:

- Decisive
- Principled
- Thorough
- Selfless

A crisis is a dramatic event for most people and applying these character traits will help keep everyone calm and allow you to make the right decisions for you and your team.

The Decision is up to You

A very wise person once explained the key elements of an outcome in this very simple formula:

$$E + R = O$$

Or more clearly stated – Event, plus Response, equals Outcome. We all have crises in our lives (our event) and we all *decide* (good, bad, or indifferent) on how to respond, and it is those two things that drive the outcome for you, your family, your team or peer group. It's a very simple yet poignant perspective on those things that happen to us. In the above equation, the only variable, or the only thing under your control, is your response. As leaders in our place of work and in our family setting, we have to respond to these crises when they arise. Doing nothing won't get the job done.

The events of September 11th, 2001 are still seared into my mind and the minds of every other American who was alive then (not to mention people around the world). The world watched as thousands of our fellow countrymen died and thousands more suffered from these heinous acts of terror. Some of us have been able to soldier on from that day. Others still mourn the death of loved ones to this very day. We all needed a leader to help us through this awful event. Early that morning on September 11th, George W. Bush, our president at the time, was in a classroom with children doing some reading activities, seemingly having a good time and enjoying the company of the teachers, students, and his staff. One of his aides came over to break the news to him that the U.S. was under attack by terrorists. I'll never forget the look on his face. He looked like most Americans did that day. Shocked. Upset. Confused. Sad.

Many Presidents have had to deal with some dreadful times. Lincoln had the Civil War, Kennedy had the Cuban Missile Crisis, Hoover had the Great Depression, but none that were so dramatic and so immediate. And whether it was out of respect or fear or whatever, Bush continued to sit in that classroom, as if completely frozen by the news. Many people were critical of his indecisiveness that day and in that moment. Why didn't he jump to action? Thank the kids for their time and then get the hell out of there and help lead us in this time of crisis? Some people look at that moment and the actions he took afterward and were very critical. But I take a slightly different viewpoint: he's a human just like the rest of us. You'd be hard pressed not to be a little stunned by that blow. I know I was...

Then Bush was able to do some things that I think showed decisiveness and leadership, which helped get our emotional mojo back after it had been beaten down so badly. In the days after 9/11, our President gave a speech to the men and women working in the danger zone at Ground Zero and to the millions of other Americans watching at home. He said we wouldn't run and hide, we wouldn't cower in the face of evil, and we would rebuild and be better and stronger than ever. Here is a brief excerpt:

> *"I want you all to know that America today, America today is on a bended knee in prayer for the people whose lives were lost here, for the workers who work here,*

for the families who mourn. The nation stands with the
good people of New York City and New Jersey and Con-
necticut as we mourn the loss of thousands of our cit-
izens....

....The nation... The nation sends its love and com-
passion to everybody who is here. Thank you for your hard
work. Thank you for makin' the nation proud, and may
God bless America."

It was genuine, it was raw, and it came from the heart and it was exactly what we needed to motivate the workers at Ground Zero in the days after this crisis. He made a decision to inspire the people of the United States so that we could start to slowly move forward from the terrible events.

After 9/11, most Americans were scared to go about anywhere. The heightened security at every major event was a reminder of the terror that was still looming out there in the shadows. We kept waiting for something bad to happen, again. A little later that year, our President attended the first game of the Major League Baseball World Series and he made the decision to throw out the first pitch. His decision to be brave and put himself in a vulnerable situation showed that we, as Americans, would not live in fear and will continue to do all the things we did before and that define our culture. We won't run. We won't cower in the face of evil. We would live our lives exactly as we had before. Sometimes leadership through a crisis doesn't need huge, grandiose decisions, but rather small, subtle touches to help get us back on track. Can the decision to inspire and be brave by simply giving a speech and throwing a baseball really make a difference in such a dramatic event? Hell yes, it can. We can save all the other politicking around the President for the talking heads, but during that time of crisis, he provided two subtle but poignant moments and it was exactly what we needed.

In my relatively short career, I have been fortunate, or unfortunate, depending on how you look at it, to experience several crises. When I first started my career, I started working for Arthur Andersen, the giant consulting and accounting firm. I was so excited to be a part of such a successful and international organization. After completing my initial training and on-boarding, I was ready to take on the world. After jumping onto my first assignment and getting a taste of the "real world," I was starting to settle in and enjoy my work and the excellent people I was working with (both clients and co-workers). And then the news broke on Enron...

At the time I had never even heard of Enron or really had any clue about what they did as a business or how our firm supported them. I did know from the press that my employer had done some suspicious accounting work at this company, and allegations were flying in from everywhere of similar activity at other clients (i.e. World-Com). We were getting daily voicemails from our CEO about how we would persevere as several of our other massive clients were starting to drop us. Before long, the company was crumbling underneath our feet, all 80,000 employees worldwide. Clients leaving the firm daily, offices closing, employees being laid off, and continued bad press coverage was a normal day. Would you say that constitutes as a crisis? As a 20-something just starting out my career, it sure felt like a crisis. I had no real experience, I had not fully established my reputation at the firm, and the company was sinking faster than the RMS Titanic. It was a scary time for many of us, but for one of my managers, it was his opportunity to shine.

One Friday morning in the spring of 2002, our practice leader was instructed to reduce the headcount of our team by two-thirds before 5 p.m. that day and with little to no more direction than that. Two-thirds of the people gone on that day. As an older professional, I still have a hard time wrapping my head around this. No time to prepare. No time to rehearse. Brutal. In a display of true leadership, he did something very unexpected. He gathered the team together in an impromptu meeting and cut through all of the rumors that had been flying around about our group. He told us honestly what he had been asked to do and asked each person to state whether they had another job offer in hand. We all knew this day was coming for a while, and several of us had already interviewed for other positions. After determining who had offers, our leader diplomatically asked if they would be okay volunteering to be one of the ones to be let go. We were able to very quickly get the team down to the slimmed down number he was asked to provide and in a very open and collaborative manner. He made the decision to be bold and open, and it saved the pain and suffering of having to look at the highest performers and go through what would normally be a very in-depth vetting process to determine who would go and who would stay. The normal rules did not apply to this situation, and he was willing to do what was best for the group to help protect us. But the leadership didn't stop there.

So now our group, down two thirds of its previous size, were hanging on for dear life to our few remaining clients. After exhausting all of his contacts at other firms to take on our team, our manager helped ensure that the remaining team members were included and cared for in the firm that ended up acquiring our group. He was so selfless that I later found out his wife pleaded with him, "So when exactly are you going to take care of your own job!?" In a time when this manager could have easily tucked his tail and run to safety and focus only on himself, his selfless decision to be bold allowed him to help turn the tides and make this crisis work out best for everyone involved. Now that is true leadership. While this approach worked out the best for everyone, there were still some folks in the group that did not like his very straight-forward and pragmatic style. They thought it was too bullish and controlling in the way he went about trying to help out the team. So while one person took the initiative to help pull the team out of a crisis and saved many from a potentially horrible situation, it did draw some ire. But we all know that making tough decisions will draw scrutiny, and we'll discuss this later in the book. As leaders, we have the strength to take the criticism because we know our family, team, and co-workers need us to step up.

Sometimes bad things are just a way of life. Murphy's Law has been around forever, and just as sure as you forget your umbrella one day, it's going to rain. As I alluded to before, in order to be an effective leader, there are always going to be some bumps in the road and your ability to handle those will define your effectiveness. Think about it from a bystander's point of view. Who do I want around to lead my team, church, or family? The person who freaks out and is indecisive when faced with a challenge, or the person who remains very calm and confident amidst the storm. I want to be led by the person that is strong and decisive coming out of bad situation. By a person who makes a decision and has a plan to get us out of this mess. By the person who cares about our team enough that they are willing to invest themselves emotionally and physically in the outcome, good, bad, or indifferent. When leading big projects or initiatives, I like to say that our success will not be defined by whether or not we make mistakes, but rather how we respond to those mistakes once they occur. Decisiveness in the face of difficulty is what defines excellent leadership. It is required. Leadership without challenge does not exist. The true definition of being a leader requires that you help your team or family through all situations, particularly the bumps, and mandates you must be decisive.

I've personally faced a whole number of crises, from sick family members to professional drama to personal challenges. Looking back over these events, it wasn't clear to me then but is very clear to me now that each crisis requires someone to step up. It's those situations when no one steps up to turn the tides it typically ends very poorly. The term *hero*, I think, is sometimes an overused and fictional word that doesn't really apply to most people. But simply stepping up within your limitations can prove to make all the difference in changing the tides of a bad situation. Even more powerful is when people unify together against this crisis to where it creates a multiplier effect to help people rise above the situation. Taking one step can make all the difference in the world.

> ...our success will not be defined by whether or not we make mistakes, but rather how we respond to those mistakes once they occur.

It may not seem like it during the moment, but like I stated before, every crisis requires a decision to turn the tides and that decision reeks of opportunity. The good news for all of us is that our crisis is finite, it will eventually end, and the decision for us is whether you want to take action and have it end positively or do nothing and have it end poorly. The choice is yours. Most of our crises are more private in nature than we think, and we also have more help than we'd ever expect. Do not do this alone. It's only on the field of play or on television where one single person is the hero or raises up the team all by their self. While I firmly believe that one person can *truly* make a difference, especially with their attitude, it doesn't *have* to just be you. Leverage the people around you and enlist others to help support your decision and turn the tide. When you get more than one person championing the same message, it makes others believe.

I said all crises require decisiveness. You need to act in order to determine the outcome. For some people, doing nothing is their "action." Many of us see bad stuff going down, whether it be bullying, poor behavior in the workplace, stealing, and any other ridiculousness you can imagine. For some of these situations, it's very apparent that something needs to be done to stop the crises, but what about the person struggling with alcoholism or struggling with an abusive co-worker or having to deal with a failing business. Don't be the person who does nothing when faced with these matters. Get help, take a stand for what you believe in but don't do nothing. You'll end up regretting it in the end.

The Principle is Your Pal

Being principled is a powerful thing. Being principled means that you are honorable, upright, ethical, and moral. It means you take the high road regardless of the situation. Being principled in a crisis is extremely difficult. Taking the easy route, or even ignoring the crisis, is much easier and free of pain. Those people that take the easy approach will ultimately fail in the end. A crisis is a time of stress and brings out the best and worst in people. It shows people's true colors. Their principles. I'll never forget people who I always considered very nice and polite suddenly acting cold and callous once Arthur Andersen started its descent. Their previously confident and strong outward appearance was replaced with their somewhat shallow and meek true inner self. Be ready to stay on your toes as you might be surprised at some people's behavior during tough times. People that you think you know will change in a heartbeat. Remember that as you lead the team out of the crisis. You will very clearly see those people with character and integrity as their true personality will show in how they act under pressure.

Principles are the same thing as your value system. Mine include treating people with respect and dignity, being positive regardless of the situation and doing the right thing all the time. It's also important to be aware of your own behavior and principles. Are you cowering in the corner or freaking out? Is that how you want to react or be remembered? Are you calm and steady when bad things happen? Try to be aware of your immediate emotions and reactions in times of stress and think about how you want people to see and remember you in those situations. The old adage of "when the going gets tough, the tough get going" is very applicable here. Those people that panic or freak out when faced with a crisis typically will perform the worst during these events and abandon their principles and values. Those that stay calm and let their moral compass be their guide will persevere more than those that do not.

Most of the standard characteristics of a crisis are negative. An illness, a layoff, a death, a loss, whatever the case might be, it is sometimes hard to look through the muck and see the positive in a crisis. But the one positive is that within any crisis lies an opportunity to exercise your principles. An opportunity to turn the tides of something bad into something good. An opportunity for you to lead your family, team, co-workers into the light when everything around you seems so dark. Like most of what is discussed in this book, it is all a matter of perspective. A crisis will typically take most people to the depths of their emotional bottom. Once you've hit the bottom, you need someone or something to help bring you back to your emotional surface and the opportunity is just that thing. While it's hard to see something so awful as a crisis as something positive, it may be just the thing that everyone around you needs to get through... don't forget that. That is character. That is principle.

No one should operate in a constant state of "crisis mode." If you have more than just a few crises in your life, you really need to go back and look at my definition above and re-calibrate your perspective and align your principles. Things like Johnny not making the varsity team, Beth scoring 40 points lower on her SATs than she should have, Dad didn't get as big a bonus last year, the kitchen tile you installed doesn't look as pretty as you thought. These are first world problems and should not be viewed as a crisis. You will drive yourself mad and deteriorate your health and well-being. You certainly *will not* enjoy the ride of life if you are constantly in this mode. Your principles will help guide you in these situations. As you reflect on those crises in your life, think over the last few years, and if you have been operating in crisis mode, don't worry. The good news is that you have likely identified your shortcomings and that is a huge self-awareness step that most are not able to accomplish.

The best way to be able to apply your principles during a crisis is being *positive*. Negativity brings out emotions which clouds your judgment and takes focus away from behaving properly. One former colleague embodied the combination of positivity and principles and had to put those to attributes to the ultimate test. This colleague was in a risk management role and through some investigation discovered significant fraudulent activities by top executives including his boss. If you knew this person, it would not surprise you that he took a stand on what he felt was right and blew the whistle on the top executive perpetuating the fraud. Most people have not had to live through a fraudulent or criminal situation, but they are some of the most stressful and intense types of crises you can encounter. This person ultimately ended up resigning for what he believed, and proved, was fraudulent behavior by the top executive. He ended up having to go in front of a judge and indict his former boss describing the wrongful behavior in court – talk about principle! Through this person's principles and high levels of integrity, he blew the whistle on this activity and person(s) involved and maintained a strong level of positivity throughout the case. Without this positive view, his principles would have crumbled and perhaps the case would have been dropped or fallen apart. This dramatic stand was able to help turn the tides in the company and help move it through a very difficult time. Want another example of facing a crisis head on and being principled? Look no further than Mark Felt….

William Mark Felt, Sr. was an investigator for the FBI from 1942 to 1973 and advanced all the way to Associate Director during his long career. While most don't recognize Felt's real name, many will recognize his nickname "Deep Throat" as he was the secret informant to the reporters at the Washington Post helping to break open the Watergate scandal. I never fully understood the details of the Watergate scandal but in effect President Richard Nixon and his top aides conducted a variety government abuses like bugging the offices of political adversaries along with several other improprieties while leveraging government agencies to do so. When word started to leak out on the misdeeds, Nixon and his aides then doubled down by trying to cover it all up. Pretty terrible government abuse which eventually led to Nixon's resignation. Felt was at the center of the leak working with the Washing Post reporters to give details of the misdeeds helping expose these government officials ultimately bringing them to justice. There has been debate amongst the political pundits on whether Felt's role in bringing down the Nixon administration was pure or whether he exposed the misdeeds to try and get a larger role at the FBI and other opportunities. However, you have to think that on some level Felt was carrying out his role, and staying anonymous until decades after the scandal, in an effort to align with his principles of right and wrong. Someone had to expose this inappropriate behavior and Felt had the courage and facts to do so.

Dealing with a crisis that impacts other people can be very tough for any leader, regardless of how many times they've been through it. The best leaders know their people, know their culture, and the environment in which they work and operate. These folks have an uncanny "feel" for the space in which they work and the ability to read and react to the always changing variables around them. Just like a top NFL quarterback can make a pinpoint pass under extreme pressure, these leaders can sift through all the noise and stick to their principles. These leaders can sift through that muck and make the right maneuver. How do they do this, and more importantly, how can you replicate that mojo without having to get decades of experience?

What these leaders know is that sometimes you need to make things that are a crisis not a crisis. Many leaders realize what their team needs to get through a crisis is not more drama, stress, and tension. What they need is serenity, peace, and clarity to help manage through. This helps individual and company principles shine through. Even despite the worst situation, these leaders are calm, poised, and professional. Now, I'm not suggesting anything but complete honesty as the guiding principle here; however, there are times when disarming something can go a long way to helping the team rally together and get out of the ditch. I try to leverage humor in these situations. I had to deliver some bad news that one project my team had spent months preparing for was getting cancelled. I knew they would be frustrated and devastated. The project was based in Asia and most of the team was based in the U.S. I organized a mandatory call on the Wednesday evening before we were supposed to leave on Friday.

I opened the call and said, "Well, guys, I have some good news and some bad news. But the good news is bad!" The team instantly knew what was happening and started cracking up. After carefully explaining the situation, everyone was somewhat relieved and accepting of the outcome. Just the same, there are times when the same leaders need to tell their team in no uncertain terms "This is bad and we need to muscle through it…and quickly."

Being truthful and candid can win respect, but balancing it without sharing everything can help you avoid panic, rumors, and gossip. If you're in a crisis and you want to downplay it, be very thoughtful and deliberate in how you do this. Confidence and reassurance can help your team maintain their principles during this time, allowing them to do their job effectively. Your assurance, along with the facts, can help strike a good balance between employees feeling comfortable but knowing they need to do more. Many times telling the team, "We aren't going to panic, we are going to be strong, team together, and communicate freely to get through this" helps create a vision for how people will act. Remember, strength and courage for the team during a time of crisis can be hugely valuable to getting through the tough times. Be thoughtful and careful on how you use this in your interactions with the team. Even if the crisis ends horribly, if you operated with high levels of integrity you can look back on the situation with pride and confidence knowing you handled the situation correctly.

Be Selfless

The next characteristic to leverage during a crisis is probably the easiest to understand but the hardest to implement. Being totally selfless in the event of crisis will help guide you to the best possible outcome for everyone involved. Very simply – being selfless requires you to think of yourself last and everyone else first. Again, another very difficult trait to adopt, but if you adopt it, you will have the best shot at overcoming a crisis and applying your principles. Ever head of Jabbar Gibson? No? What about Hurricane Katrina…

Hurricane Katrina was one of the worst natural disasters in U.S. history. On August 29th, 2005, the hurricane made landfall in the city of New Orleans as a Category 3 hurricane, and at its peak, had sustained winds of 170+ miles per hour. The ensuing damage and fatalities resulted after the city levees failed to operate and the city was crippled by the flood, causing billions of dollars of damage and impacting all its citizens, but the poor and homeless population of New Orleans suffered the most. An estimated 1,800 lives were lost. People were stranded on rooftops, death and destruction was all around. It was an epic crisis.

Jabbar Gibson, then a resident of New Orleans, made a decision that was truly selfless. Despite being just 18-years-old, Jabbar had a criminal record littered with several arrests, a bi-product of the tough streets in which he grew up. Jabbar made a truly selfless decision, one that could have very easily landed him back in the "big-house." He decided to steal a school bus and drive some stranded citizens to safety in Houston, TX, where they could get food and shelter. He had nothing really to gain and a TON to lose. Furthermore, the passengers of the bus had to pass around a hat to try to get gas money in order to make it all the way there. This story is an illustration of the fact that doing good things in a selfless manner for others is critical to success, especially in a crisis. It also teaches us that sometimes we need to take a risk in our decisions to rise above the crisis.

When you put self-preservation, or your personal goals, above the good of the team, you're destined to fail. When my old boss was in the middle of the Arthur Anderson meltdown, he was totally selfless, and this built an unbelievable amount of trust and leadership towards him coming out of that debacle. It also led to the new organization's culture and his leadership role that was formed out of the ashes of that experience. Don't ever forget that; to a fault, be selfless.

Aside from your ability to be decisive in the face of a crisis, it's also critical to be able to identify the crisis. You are able to do this when you are selfless and thinking about others beyond yourself. Those focused on themselves are too inward to notice these crises coming at them. Overlooking something that is significant can allow the crisis to go on long enough to where no matter how decisive you are, it's too late. When the ship was going down back when I was working for Arthur Anderson, there were lots of signs for all of us working there that the iceberg was coming. We were getting calls from our CEO, emails from other leaders, support from media relations folks, all of which we'd never received before. I took these cues to update my resume or prepare myself for what was likely inevitable because, at that point, I was very selfish. Instead of thinking of the company, I thought of myself. What if I had tried to save a few clients or produce better work during this critical time? Could I have saved some peoples' jobs? It's hard to say, but we'll never know because I did not take the correct path in this crisis. So when the inevitable happened and the company went under, I was hit with a major personal crisis. I wasn't an established senior leader yet, but if I was, imagine the impact of my selfishness. I could have been jeopardizing the livelihood of all my employees, potentially impacting people's ability to put food on the table, a roof over their head, sending their children to school, and so on. I was being selfish. Dealing with and identifying these crises is very important and can break apart an otherwise successful career in the blink of an eye. Keep your eyes open all the time and don't let naivety get the best of you.

The old adage that "imitation is the sincerest form of flattery" is true when dealing with a crisis. Families and professional teams look to the leaders to determine how they should act in certain situations. Whether you like it or not, if you are in a leadership position (whether you view yourself as a leader or not), people will look to you and imitate how you act. This innate element of human nature is something hard-wired in our psyche, and whether we like it or not, it's a fact of life. If my kids see me freak out at the first sign of tough times, you can bet your arse that they will imitate that the second they encounter something similar. Several years ago, when our first child was learning how to walk, she would frequently fall and stumble as she learned to gain her balance. A few times she would fall on her face or land really hard. Each time she wouldn't really react until she saw the look of fear and anxiety on her parents' face running to help her up. When she saw our fearful reaction, she knew, even at a young age, that she was supposed to have been much more upset. She would eventually see our reaction and cry and wail to match it. It took us until child number three that we really learned to be composed and calm when the kiddo would fall and scrape their knee or get hurt, and in almost every case, they would follow suit. Although a juvenile example, most adults will take a similar path as an infant when faced with a crisis and look to leaders on how to react, so it always helps to be aware of your reaction and be selfless. As much as we like to believe that people around us listen to what we say and obey those orders, the reality is that they watch what we do and follow. Remember that. People watch what we do and follow. Being selfless will allow them to also do so and work for the betterment of the situation.

Sometimes, even despite your best efforts, a crisis is just going to end badly. Do what is right for all the people involved and you will be able to have a clean conscience. Sometimes when you know the situation is going to crash and burn, it might feel like walking away from it is the right thing to do. Or even worse, not tell anyone. Many people will see a difficult situation or crisis and not tell anyone in fear that it might reflect poorly on *them*. When you know of a crisis, especially one that won't end well, it shows that you are principled and selfless to let others know and ask for help. In my career I have had to tell senior leaders that we weren't going to achieve a milestone, we had major personnel issues, we

> Remember that. People watch what we do and follow.

were over budget, I was unhappy in a role, and a myriad of other difficult items. In every situation where I dealt with it directly, honestly, and openly, I received help and we managed through the issue. Those situations where I took shortcuts by being selfish typically ended up very poorly. Transparency and honesty with what is going on, the likely outcome of the situation and offering to help can only position you as a caring leader who is looking out for their people in this difficult time. It is easy to be self-serving in this situation, but that will only get you so far. Bringing awareness to the major issue will not only ensure a positive outcome, but it will pay big dividends in other ways.

Just like it's important to emulate the right behaviors when faced with adversity, it's equally important to take action. Being selfish and doing nothing can be a big blow to your potential endeavors within an organization and can seriously impede your ability to move upward and onward.

Think about it this way. People who manage others are constantly looking for ways to better the organization and for people who have the ability to help move the company forward in the face of challenges. When it's time for you to be promoted, your boss will look at what you achieved or accomplished during your career and will most certainly ask about circumstances that were tough and challenging. If those circumstances for you involved you sitting on the sidelines and not getting into the game, it is not going to play well for you.

Not only can inaction in the face of a crisis hurt you from a long-term perspective in your career, it can hurt your personal life as well. Take a risk and run toward the fire, not away from it. Inaction in the face of crisis can send a strong message to those who count on you. I've heard the expression that it's very easy to be married on vacation but very hard to be married in the face of real-world crises. People who run away at those times let everyone down and are selfish. You invest time and energy with these trusted people in your life, and the thought of inaction in the face of a challenge will not only be a slap in the face, but also be a potential fatal flaw in the relationship. That loved one might think, "They don't care about me when it counts and when I need them the most." Get involved in your friends' and family's life. They won't forget it and you will definitely feel better about yourself the more selfless you are.

Great leaders believe in themselves enough to step into the spotlight during very cloudy times and calmly and coolly lead their teams back to a state of normal. Anyone can lead during "normal" times. Excellent leaders can seamlessly lead their teams during tough times, and the reason they can do this is through being selfless. They don't see their tough circumstances as a burden but rather an opportunity. A chance for them to do their thing during crunch time. A crisis can be the watershed moment of a career or life, for better or for worse, and that's why it matters.

Thoroughly Amused

I had to learn the hard way about the pace at which I move through a crisis. My nature is often to be impatient when I feel the pressure of a crisis weighing down on me. For the longest time, I was very quick to jump toward the solution and get on to quickly implementing change, whatever it was. I would do whatever it would take to make the pain go away as fast possible. This mindset almost got me into real trouble on one particular occasion.

Several years ago, my team was engaged to help revive a distressed project. We walked into the situation knowing it was bad and very close to being cancelled after years of work and millions of dollars being spent. It was a full-out dumpster fire. I was not the sole leader of our team, but I was one of the first lieutenants leading a major workstream. My job was to take this workstream of the project, assess it, and figure out a way to get it back on track and then report up to our project leader and the client. True to form, I rapid-fire blasted through a handful of interviews, reviewed a few documents, and then came up with recommendations on how to get that sucker back on track. A project they had been working on for years and I had figured it out in a week. I had it *all* figured out. We'd have this thing back on track in no time and they'd carry me down Main Street on their shoulders with a ticker tape parade.

When I brought my findings and recommendations back to the team, I was certain everyone would be impressed with my work and that they would be finished with their analysis as well. I was astonished to find our project leader was barely just getting ramped up on his piece and still had many interviews left to conduct. He asked me a few simple questions about my report, and it was apparent that my work was incomplete. But I was confused: this project was on fire, we were charging by the hour, and this client needed and expected results right away. A crisis brings pain and most people want the pain to end as soon as possible. Why didn't anyone have a high sense of urgency here?!

In this special circumstance, what was required was patience, diligence, and very thoughtful next steps... not speed. Very thoughtful next steps and decision-making is hugely paramount in any crisis. Every crisis requires a decision, and in getting to the crisis, there have been a whole host of poor decisions made, likely in haste, to get into the current difficult situation. Don't make that same mistake. Be slow and carefully examine the decisions and structure that was put into place that got the team to the bad spot they are in today. Being creative and unconventional but slow in your decisions will likely yield the best results when the norm has not worked to date. *Move slow to move fast...*

There's another reason why moving slowly is important, other than for making good decisions. There are many books written about change and its effect on people and organizations. The phrase "velocity of change" is a cool consultant type term that folks latch onto and use far too frequently. Velocity of change is how quickly you and your team are able to accept and absorb something new. Most of the time, when there are really big initiatives across an organization, there is a tremendous focus put on change management. When there is a crisis, your organization, family, church, or team gets hit with a double whammy of change. Things likely aren't going well for some reason, so there are some serious emotional impacts and changes, in addition to whatever process or procedural changes you as a leader are about to implement to get the team out of the crisis. Be very careful to remember that to move slowly and thoughtfully when making any changes.

In Summary

Crises will happen in your life regardless of what you do to prevent or avoid them. Stuff happens. Period. Most leaders are defined by how they perform during the tough times. Sometimes people are remembered by leading through the good times, but if you're a leader, you know nothing ever goes perfectly smooth. Embrace the tough times; they are your opportunities to enrich your team and your career. To be a proven leader, you have to lead through adversity and your ability to do so will define your career and the trajectory of your success. Embracing it is your only real option!

LTF Action Plan:

1. Make a tough decision in your next crisis
2. Do the right thing, every time
3. Forget about yourself in the next crisis
4. Slow down on the worst things

Chapter 6 – Personal Attack

Andy was a rising star in the consulting world. Andy was good-looking, well-dressed, polished, and a natural born leader that everyone gravitated towards. He came from a blue-collar family in the mid-west and carried a part-time job from the time he was 13. He worked hard his entire life and was a sharp guy who climbed the ladder at his firm quickly, based on his pure grit and determination. Andy played varsity football in high-school, graduated as vale-dictorian, and ended up going to an ivy league school on a full scholarship where he majored in economics and was at the top of his class. Now working for a top consulting firm, Andy was a strong-willed person and always did his best, regardless of the circumstances. As a working professional, Andy was active in his church, volunteered in his community, and visited his grand-mother regularly in the nursing home. He was truly the all-American boy and had achieved high levels of success at a very young age. He was on track to become partner of his firm earlier than anyone in its 100+ year history.

Despite his pristine image and meteoric rise to the top, Andy kept getting pulled aside by the senior partners of the firm. Several of his peers had come to the top leadership of the firm to complain about Andy. One person complained about his style and approach (too aggressive). Another about his attitude (too positive). Still, another about his appearance being too polished (yes, his appearance!). After a short conversation with each of the senior leaders, he was able to easily dismiss these claims against him, but after the fourth instance, he started to get paranoid. Even with some of these "escalations," Andy's team was consistently high performing, on time, and on budget with his projects. He was viewed as a star by the client and the higher up leaders at the firm. He even went out of his way to build strong relationships with his peers and just could not fathom why he was getting all this bad press from them. Despite the consistent success on the job, the rumors and whispers grew louder and louder. The stories and personal attacks continued, even to the point where he contemplated leaving the firm altogether. He knew all of the personal attacks weren't based on anything real, but the emotional roller coaster was taking a toll on him. He eventually got to the point where he had to decide between quitting the firm or being confident in his leadership skills and instincts and continue to do what he knew in his heart was right...

++++

There's an interesting phenomenon that happens when you move up the ranks as a leader: a long line of people want to take personal shots at you. Whether it be about your decisions, managerial style, your clothes, your team, the car you drive, or anything else under the sun, you are going to be subjected to petty, personal attacks. Consider this phenomenon something that comes with leadership. Trying to change it is a waste of your time and can lead to frustration. Haters gonna hate, so go ahead and let them. The real thing to think about is what are you going to do about these attacks when they occur? Are you going to do anything? *Should* you do anything? These are all questions that every leader will have to think through when the personal attacks come along.

So what exactly is a personal attack anyway? It's a negative story about a leader, which may or may not be based on facts. It is driven by emotion and is normally disparaging against the target. In its simplest form, it's somebody taking a shot at you because of who you are and the position you hold (and jealousy!). Interestingly, most of the time, these personal attacks get to you second or third hand from the instigator. Very rarely does someone have the courage or stupidity to launch this attack directly to your face. They'd rather whisper it in the shadows to a peer or spout off about it on social media. This makes the rumor or attack more difficult to accept because you sometimes don't know exactly where it's coming from and it's two to three steps removed. When someone attacks you, it can have a real negative impact to your psyche if you aren't prepared for it or have the confidence to dismiss it.

No one knows this success and personal attack dynamic more than NFL coaches. From the department of neurotic people, we present to you, the NFL fan. There are countless examples where an NFL coach has had great success on the field and is then later run out of town by the impatient and unreasonable fans or general manager of the team. The list is long.

Coach Jon Gruden won Super Bowl XXXVII for the Tampa Bay Buccaneers, a franchise long known for their lack of winning teams. The Bucs had a lifetime of little to no success on the gridiron. They have been awful since their inception and considered a poorly run franchise. Finally, after years of failures, they found a coach who could put together a winning combination on the field and bring hope to a fan base who had never experienced a legitimate contender. How did they treat Gruden's on the field success after his Super Bowl win? By firing him a few years later, that's how. And it wasn't just wins and losses, they criticized his scowl, his demeanor in interviews and press conferences, and everything else in between. They got personal. Granted there were some challenges with the team and their ability to produce a winner since the Super Bowl victory, but it didn't take long for the tides to turn and that was all she wrote for Jon. Want another example? Try Mike Shanahan.

Mike Shanahan won two Super Bowls in Denver and brought the Lombardi trophy back to a franchise that had been to the championship game several times but was never able to bring home the big prize. Prior to Mike coming along, the Broncos had the franchise quarterback of a generation in John Elway and a damn fine football coach in Dan Reeves, but they just couldn't get it done on the field. Shanahan came in with his solid running attack and stellar defense and they won two titles toward the end of Elway's career, when you could argue that the hall of famer's skills were diminishing. After his years of success, the luster started to wane. Once considered *the* mastermind of the gridiron, his mental faculties were challenged. His skill and instinct as a coach called into question and attacked. Some even said the game had passed him by. It got personal. Shanahan was eventually canned for low performance after bringing the franchise years of unbridled success. The NFL is a success-based business. You win, you get rewarded, but sometimes it gets personal when things aren't going as expected.

Need more? How about Mike Ditka, Brian Billick, Don McCafferty; the list goes on and on. Maybe the NFL coaching profession is not the best example to use because of its inherent precariousness, but the point is that even though you can have great success, the haters will still come out if you slip even the slightest bit. They are waiting to pounce. It's a performance based world out there, and NFL coaches have a bullseye on them at all times. You should expect that and prepare for it as you become a leader for your team as well.

Look no further than the political landscape for some of the absolute craziest personal attacks you can imagine. Anyone who has a television knows when it's getting close to election time because the personal attack TV commercials start coming out of the woodwork. While these ridiculous ads are a relatively new thing, taking cheap shots at your political opponent has certainly been around for a long time. Political personal attacks date back to some of the earliest recorded history ("Et tu Brute?"as Julius Caesar might say). During the 1828 presidential campaign, Andrew Jackson's opponent, John Quincy Adams, launched what is assumed to be the first organized personal political attack in the United States by launching the Coffin Handbills. The Coffin Handbills were a series of pamphlets written and distributed with the focus on attacking Jackson due to his interactions and involvement in the War of 1812. Adams vilified Jackson as a brutal killer of innocent Native Americans and other soldiers. The personal attacks allegedly got so bad that Jackson's mother was accused of being a prostitute and his wife not much better. Talk about hitting below the belt!

Lyndon Johnson used the "Daisy Ad" as a way to personally attack his opponent, Barry Goldwater, in the 1964 Presidential election. The Daisy Ad showed a young girl in a meadow playing with a flower when a nuclear launch countdown and explosion floods the screen with dramatic imagery. Many speculate this personal attack on Goldwater's weak military stance, which hit on the very real fear about nuclear weapons during this Cold War era, helped lead to Johnson's landslide victory. The "Harry and Louise" ads were used as personal attacks against Bill Clinton for his proposed controversial health care plan in 1993, which is eerily familiar to some of the rhetoric thrown around on "Obamacare." Not to be outdone, a 2005 gubernatorial race had a pro-death penalty ad trying to slander one of the opponents, but it ended up backfiring and resulted in the candidate losing the race (the ad also invoked an image of Hitler, which is never really a good idea if you want to try and get yourself elected).

I have never understood the thinking behind using personal attacks to try to win a political campaign, or any other internal corporate political jockeying for that matter. Besides making the attacker look juvenile and childish, if your main strategy for trying to succeed is based on making your opponent look like a buffoon, then maybe you should consider getting a better strategy. Perhaps one based on your own merit? Again, I digress...

As a leader, you get paid to deal with stress and make tough decisions, all of which come with high levels of scrutiny and personal attacks. You need to be ready to deal with these bumps as they will arise regardless of your circumstances because they just simply are going to occur. Ignoring it or being surprised by the personal attack as a leader (at any level) is totally on you. It's going to happen, so you might as well be prepared. Being prepared puts you in a position of strength vs. a position of weakness where you are having to react and are not prepared. Don't be the leader that's not prepared or surprised by these attacks.

In any personal attack on your character, there are several elements to consider and manage to not let it get the better of you. Like many of the other bumps you come across, to make it work, you need high levels of discipline and focus. For each personal attack, you will have to come to grips with the following:

- Your emotions
- Perception vs. Reality
- Confidence

Mastering each of these will help make sure that the personal attackers don't get the best of you and you can continue on your leadership journey with success.

Time to Get Emotional

When someone attacks you personally, there are so many emotions that can arise. Anger. Frustration. Regret. Wonder. Hatred. You name it, all the ugly ones come rushing to the surface. But they are all *natural* reactions when an attack hits right at the core of who you are. That's the good news. The bad news is that it doesn't change anything about the situation, and the hatred and anger is still there because some moron was totally out of line and didn't know what the hell they were talking about. I digress. The key thing about the emotions that stem from a personal attack is that they can cloud your judgment. Make you do things you otherwise would not do under duress. Acting out of character can make the personal attack a situation where you are also reflected poorly in the situation.

It hurts when someone says something bad about you, whether it's true or not. Take the story of Andy at the beginning of this chapter. If he would have calmed himself down and addressed these attacks directly, he likely would have continued on his meteoric rise up the corporate ladder. If you are a leader, you are undoubtedly strong in your conviction and have a good sense of who you are, but it still stings when someone takes a shot at you.

You might ask, "Why is this happening to me?"

"Why would they make that up?"

"Why does everyone hate me?" When someone hits you in the nose for no reason, you need to ask a whole set of other questions and these are the ones that really count.

I had a personal attack from a peer in a prior job that really got the best of me. This person was attacking my intelligence and work ethic, and for whatever reason, those two areas are major hot buttons for me. I found out what was being said about me through a peer. It was like someone punched me in the gut. What was being said was not true, and furthermore, was getting around to more than one person. I was pissed. I found this out in the workplace walking in between meetings and had to walk outside for a few minutes to cool off. I was literally concerned I might become violent or lash out at this person or even others who had heard the story. It rocked my emotions. I was mostly angry and went home several days in a row venting to my wife and in a majorly sour mood. Several days. My emotions were a mess and got the best of me.

I finally addressed the issue and was able to move on but was furious for several days. Yes, I have a temper! It wasn't until talking to a buddy that he really helped set me straight. He said that my emotions were clouding how I looked at the whole situation. The person that was launching the personal attack was a known low performer and someone who constantly stirred things up at work. This "ankle-biter" was getting the best of me and I didn't even realize it.

My good buddy said bluntly, "You're letting your emotions run wild." He was right. For whatever reason, I was letting my insecurities cloud the fact that I was a high performer with an established reputation and a track record of success. Who really cared what the known trouble-maker had to say. I was a known quantity and considered very reliable and trustworthy. Why would anyone even believe the things that were being said?

As a leader, when the personal attack comes, it will trigger emotions. Sometimes it will make you laugh because the story or attack is so ridiculous. Beyond everything else, if you don't control your emotions when the personal attacks come, you will not handle them well. Again, if you don't control your emotions when faced with personal attacks, the outcome will not be good. Someone once created a yarn about my attire and that it wasn't professional. Ha! In some cases, the personal attack can make us feel sorrow for the other person. These attackers clearly have interpersonal issues and are lashing out at those that are successful. Why would someone say that or do that to me?

Personal attacks that create humor, sorrow, or wonder are something most of us can overlook. It doesn't immediately spurn us to act but rather reflect on the situation; it isn't a threat to us. It is really one emotion that you'll need to manage when the attack is launched and that is *anger*. Anger is a very hard emotion to contain. Anger causes you to react and to react without thinking about the consequences. Anger can get you into trouble and you should expect the outcomes to be bad. If you know it's coming, then you should be able to contain your anger and specifically prevent yourself from over-reacting. But if you cannot control your anger, then you will react, and sometimes it can be UGLY.

If there ever was a case where personal attacks got the emotions (anger) running high, it was the 2008 U.S. Senate race in North Carolina. The race pitted incumbent Elizabeth Dole against upstart Kay Hagan in a hotly contested battle over the important senate seat. Dole was the incumbent and doing everything to hang onto her seat in congress against the back-drop of a major recession and the low approval rating of then President George W. Bush. Elizabeth Dole was married to one-time Presidential candidate Bob Dole but was no political slouch herself. She was a graduate of Duke University and Harvard Law School and served as the Secretary of Labor *and* Secretary of

Transportation under two different presidents, and she was head of the American Red Cross even before her political career started up. Pretty big deal, right? She had served as U.S. Senator for the great state of North Carolina for five years and won her seat by becoming the first female senator from North Carolina back in 2003. She had a strong resume, was very intelligent, and had proven political chops.

Kay Hagan was an underdog candidate. A NC state senator from Greensboro who also had a strong show of support from then Presidential candidate Barack Obama. The race ended up being highly contested until Dole made the mistake of taking a personal attack too far. With North Carolina being in the heart of the "Bible Belt," any accusations around religion should be done so very carefully and with extreme caution for the threat of potential backlash. Dole made the decision to air a personal attack TV ad against Hagan because of her alleged acceptance of donations from "Godless Americans PAC." The ad showed a picture of Hagan with a female voice overdub saying, "There is no God," insinuating that these words were part of her belief system. Whoa, Elizabeth! Going straight for the jugular, aren't ya? The ad insinuated that the church-going, former Sunday School teacher (literally) did not believe in God. Pretty steep accusations for anyone, and there was such a backlash (anger) from the personal attack that Dole's campaign basically imploded upon itself. Hagan won by the widest margin in North Carolina in over 30 years, the largest margin of defeat for an incumbent in that year's election. Was the ridiculous personal attack the sole reason for the defeat? Likely not, but it probably had some role in the downfall and hit on emotions that turned the tide of the race. A personal attack can trigger some strong emotions on both sides of the coin, and for that reason, we need to slow down and address our emotions before we proceed. Slowly and confidently addressing these attacks, without emotion, can help address the concerns that are there. Reacting without emotion will make all the difference in your response and how you process and adjust to those attacks and your ability to keep you emotions in check.

The unfortunate reality is that the higher up on the food chain you go on your road to success, the more the personal attacks will occur. If you're Joe Blow in accounting, then there's probably not a lot of people who are lining up to bitch and complain about you or nit-pick how you do things. However, if you are Shawna Smith, CEO, then there is a long line of people who will make up stories about you right, wrong or indifferent. It's just a fact of life. Now people will also gossip and tell stories about the receptionist or salesperson, you just won't see it in the same way you would for the CEO.

When it comes to a personal attack, all bets are off. You can throw the rule book out the window and expect that your emotions are going to run high. You can take all the good advice and perspective from your colleagues, read a bunch of books on the topic, but when it happens to you…it's a different story. So while I will preach preparation and planning, the bottom line is that until you get hit with it, you don't really know how you'll react. Or as Mike Tyson once quipped, "Everyone has a plan until they get punched in the mouth." It's the same way with a personal attack, you have to experience it before you know your natural reaction. Regardless of the situation and emotion that is triggered, you will have a reaction, and whether that is good or bad is mostly based on time.

You might be surprised by your behavior when the first grenade gets launched in your direction. Depending on who you are, you might laugh. Some cry. Even others get angry. In the end, you will either do one of two things:

- React
- Overreact

Typically, when you over-react, it is immediate. The overreactions come from anger and those emotions that are difficult to control. Reactions, on the other hand, are those that are tied to emotions that are easier to control. Humor. Wonder. Pity. These emotions don't cause the immediate, neg-

...the way you respond is infinitely more important than how quickly you respond.

ative response to the personal attack. Because they aren't as raw and personal, it allows you think more carefully about the circumstance and take the *correct* path forward. The secret in all of this is that once you get your first personal attack, you will want to react swiftly and with emotion – don't. React slowly. Take your time. Make the right move and not the emotional move. It's easier said than done, but it makes all the difference in overcoming the personal attack. Make the decision now that when someone attacks, you will move slowly and without emotion (anger) in dealing with your first personal attack. Being able to apply some of the principles noted above becomes increasingly difficult if you are filled with emotion and anger. Let the emotion pass and make the right move for your situation. Acting on emotion will more than likely get the wrong result every time. As a young person, I always wanted to move fast and react to every little thing that came my way – personal attack or not. I am still like that in some ways today. It took me a long time to realize that the way you respond is infinitely more important than how quickly you respond. Let that be a lesson to me and any of those us out there willing to listen.

I was on a high-profile project one time and had a very high performing, hard charging, direct report. This person, Larry, was type A all around. Got into the details, could problem solve on the fly, and really drove results. Larry was awesome. He was a tactician but also a great communicator and salesman. One day on project, his peer Ellen came storming into my office. Didn't knock. Didn't ask if now was a good time. Came right in sat down and started to unload. "Larry did this, Larry did that." On and on, yelling about Larry and what he had done. Of course I was intimately involved in the project and knew a lot of Ellen's gripes were second hand and totally incorrect. It was honestly hilarious. The claims were so emotion-filled that it was clear this person was angry and not thinking clearly. The person then pivoted to critiquing me. That was a mistake. She said I could not manage, had no control over my team, and on and on. Again, because the whole thing was so ridiculous, it didn't even make me mad. I calmly listened, and once she ran out of breath, I systematically refuted, with facts, each of her points. Because I controlled my emotions on the matter, I did not overreact on the situation, and in turn, the outcome was much better. Your reaction to the personal attack will determine the outcome.

So, what do you do about the attack? Let it get under your skin or motivate you? As a leader, you are likely prone to taking action. The key is to determine what direction your action is going to follow – negative or positive. Lots of people take negative things others say about them or their teams and companies and use that as a motivating factor for them. I've never been one to use hatred or anger to get me motivated, but some people thrive on the underdog role and thinking that the world is out to get them. Having someone think they can't do something makes them want to prove the haters wrong, and it really helps to bring out their best performance. Whatever the case might be for you, think carefully about the personal attack and whether it can help you in some way.

Perception or Reality?

So who really cares if someone shoots some proverbial arrows your way? I mean, that person has no idea what really went into a decision or all the considerations that go into why you do things a certain way. Why even consider their jabs at all? What if some of the personal attacks on you were *true*?

So, why are personal attacks relevant? One, they can diminish your ability to perform at a high level and erode the time you spend each day doing those things that are important. They distract. Secondly, in some cases, the attack can be real. You may have a flaw or improvement area that you do

> If you're not careful and you let them go on long enough, they can start to become reality.

need to clean up. Robert Kiyosaki said it best when he said, "Critics only make you stronger. You have to look at what they are saying as feedback. Sometimes the feedback helps, and other times, it's just noise that can be a distraction."

Whether the attack is real or not, here's another reason why you should care about personal attacks. If you're not careful and you let them go on long enough, they can start to become reality. Think about that. If enough people start to spread a rumor about you, then it starts to become *your* story and shape other people's opinions of you. For example, if people didn't know you but heard you were difficult to work with and very tough on your direct reports, that story might start to stick if not proven wrong by your actions and behaviors. By sticking, I mean that people would start to assume you *are* like that, even if it's true or not. Before you know it, when people meet you for the first time, they may have their guard up or not be their true self around you because of a pre-conceived belief they have about you. So before you know it, this personal attack has become who you are, whether you like it or not. Perception has become reality.

I had a co-worker who was viewed as a jerk by his peers and direct reports. I've known a lot of jerks in my personal and professional life, this guy was not a jerk. He was a good family man, very smart but also very passionate and stubborn. As someone who is also very stubborn, I understood him and saw past his stubbornness and could see his better traits but was one of only a few people who did. I distinctly remember him arguing with someone seven years his junior over a mundane topic for 35 minutes. In a conference room. In front of everyone. I pulled him aside after the very visible argument and asked what the heck he was doing. I agreed with him that the junior team member should have listened and tried to "learn something," but as a leader, he had to be better than that. After this altercation and several others that were similar in nature, my buddy almost lost his job when there was a mutiny during his stint as an office lead. Again, the guy made it to office lead because he was *really* good, but he almost got fired because of the personal attacks on his style and approach. The personal attacks *became* reality! I'm not suggesting that you need to chase down and disprove every personal attack that comes your way but rather be aware of them and let your actions and behaviors shape others' perception of you. Perception is reality for many people, and if you let the personal attack take shape, then that story will be *you* to those that don't know *you*. Weird, huh?

Simply knowing that many of the personal attacks are not based in reality but based in jealousy and people's own shortcomings can help you have perspective on what to take seriously and what to ignore. Does the person doling out the personal attack have legitimate motivation for providing an attack? Reality? The reality is that some people just like to complain no matter what. Things could be going great in every aspect of their lives, yet they just like to complain and whine. But maybe you could even take the personal attack as a way to coach and mentor the attacker. Turn lemons into lemonade. Maybe that person has a challenge or is frustrated and you might be in a position to help them. This personal attack might be a cry for help. What a great opportunity to take the high road and help someone else in their leadership journey by providing them some perspective. Again, consider the source and know who you should pay attention to and who you should not and you'll be much better off.

The idea that if you're walking around saying yes to everyone you encounter or giving them exactly what they want you might be doing them and yourself a disservice and likely never have anyone ever attack you. As we covered in the nemesis chapter, you shouldn't go around looking for fights or to become enemies with everyone around you but pushing back and ruffling some feathers, only on occasion, is not always a bad thing. The dirty little secret here is that if you're encountering personal attacks, you are most likely being decisive and making critical moves that are helping advance your organization, family, and your career. Being decisive and making moves is not an easy thing to do and is a huge milestone in your career. The act of making a decision implies there is more than one path to take and that you chose one that seemed the best based on the facts, your experience, and insight. In making those decisions and moves, there are sometimes going to be some repercussions. The old saying you can't make an omelet without breaking a few eggs is pretty applicable here.

You should take comfort that you are making moves and not sitting idly on the sidelines. Not everyone is going to love every move you make as a leader. If you weren't making a difference in the organization, you likely would be hearing nothing on the personal attack front. The other secret here is that if the silence is deafening around what you are doing, then perhaps you aren't being decisive enough and making the right moves. If there are no personal attacks, you should also be concerned! How about that! Surely there is a long list of people who have never encountered a personal attack and are wildly successful leaders. There is something to be said for being liked. But as the famous quote from Laurel Thatcher Ulrich goes, "Well-behaved women seldom make history." I love this quote but think it applies to everyone. Don't be a pain in the arse but also don't be afraid to make decisions, even tough ones that go against the grain. Your best weapon in helping navigate a personal attack is the helpful tool of confidence.

Confidence

The one trump card all of us have over the personal attack is confidence. If you are confident, you believe in yourself. Because you believe in yourself, you rarely have anger-filled reactions to the personal attack. Because you don't get angry, you typically don't overreact. And because you don't overreact, any perceptions are managed. Confidence is the single thread throughout that can help you manage the situation. Will the personal attack change how you do things or will it shake your confidence? The personal attack should certainly not shake your confidence. There will always be bumps in the road to success, and personal attacks will be a dime a dozen once you've done anything

> Being comfortable with being uncomfortable is a skill that most leaders master and it just becomes part of the fabric of their being.

in your career, especially if you are a little different or unique. Having the will to be strong and passionate, even in the face of disparaging words, is something you have to get comfortable with in your career. Being comfortable with being uncomfortable is a skill that most leaders master and it just becomes part of the fabric of their being. They think, "Well, this has never happened to me before, but I'm up for the challenge!" It doesn't shake their confidence and they've learned that haters will come and go, but if they stick hard and fast to their ideals and principles, then they will overcome whatever gets thrown at them.

Some people take the approach that they just don't care what others think or say about them. This is executive presence, a high level display of confidence. The ability to not get caught up in the petty day to day insecurities of others. It is a mindset and one most truly great leaders possess. It is impossible to chase away all the haters, but a balance of having confidence in yourself and knowing who you are, while also dismissing the personal attacks, is a good place to focus. No one knows the constant hate and rhetoric like John Calipari.

John Vincent Calipari is a basketball coach who formerly coached in the NBA and is now the head coach of the University of Kentucky Wildcats. Those who are not University of Kentucky basketball fans think of him as a "cheater" because at his two prior college head coaching jobs (UMass and Memphis), they had to vacate wins due to NCAA infractions.

At UMass, Coach Cal led his team to the NCAA final four where they lost in the semi-final game to the University of Kentucky in 1996. UMass had to vacate wins because one of Coach Cal's star players from that team, Marcus Camby, accepted a gift from a sports agent. Clearly this was against the rules, making Marcus ineligible for the games he played while wearing a UMass uniform. If you're a Coach Cal hater, you say, "He was the head coach of the program, he should have known and prevented that type of behavior and not re-cruited certain kids." If you're a coach Cal fan, you say "How can he supervise the kids every second of the day and prevent all of the temp-tations that swirl around high-profile student-athletes?" Regardless of the camp in which you reside, Cal *could* have certainly gone after Marcus Camby in the name of self-preservation to protect his own credibility and try to get another coaching job. After all, it was Marcus that took the improper benefit, right? Not Cal.

What Coach Cal ended up doing was the total opposite. He aligned himself to Marcus and is a staunch defender of him to this day. He maintains a deep relationship with him and still talks highly about Marcus. Coach Cal was confident in who he is and the kind of person that Marcus is as well.

What about Coach Cal's career at Memphis? He also took that team to the final four and ended up losing to the University of Kansas in the final game of the 2008 NCAA tournament. In a very similar situation to UMass, Cal had a first team all-American player in Der-rick Rose, who was an amazing collegiate athlete. Rose led the Tigers to steamroll their way into the NCAA finals behind 38 wins, which was a season record. After Cal's team logged 38 wins that year to lose in the finals to Kansas, they had to vacate those wins because it was uncovered that Derrick Rose had an invalidated SAT test score. Spec-ulation was that Rose had someone take the test for him. Goodbye, 38 wins. Goodbye, Final Four. Again, similar to the UMass situation, Coach Cal could have attacked Rose as he had a terrible lapse in judg-ment (allegedly), and in some ways, betrayed his coach. Instead Coach Cal is fiercely loyal to Derrick to this day and keeps him in his inner circle. Cal has been attacked about the vacated wins relentlessly, and he consistently relays that he did nothing wrong but doesn't dwell on it and normally deflects the questions. Is he hiding from these allega-tions or does he know the truth and confident in that he continues to do things the "right way?" Regardless of your feelings about Cal, love him or hate him, he is supremely confident in himself and able to dismiss the constant personal attacks on his character.

How do you deal with personal attacks? Do you react appropriately? What emotions does that attack bring out in you? What decisions do you make about the attack? How does it affect the folks around you? These are all good questions to consider and reflect upon when the personal attacks come your way. To think about it slightly differently, think about the above questions and how they impact others who you are attacking. What do you mean, how *I* attack others? I wouldn't do that?! Actually, you would and you do attack others but probably don't even realize it. Sometimes we are so inwardly focused about how others are treating us, we forget how we behave toward them. I would be willing to bet that every one of us reading this book has perpetuated a personal attack on someone else. That's right, you're not perfect, and acting holier than thou is not a good way to act toward your peers, coworkers, or family. I'll never forget driving around the mall parking lot during Christmas time and getting aced out by another driver for a prime parking spot. I launched into a tirade about how that person was rude and lacked the Christmas spirit and how could they sleep at night for being so soulless... ridiculous, I know. I insulted this person's intelligence and called them names. Well, sure as instant karma can be said, the tables were turned. In my anger, I aced out another driver who was sitting there with their turn signal on waiting for a spot. Talk about being a hypocrite. The dust wasn't even settled on my personal attack against the other driver, and here I was, acting out on some other poor soul. The first rule of being able to deal with a personal attack is to be void of that tendency yourself. Being strong enough to not attack others who are better, smarter, or more talented than you is the first step to being able to deal with the hate that comes your way. Don't be a hater!

If I am honest with myself, I find that I think some not-so-great things about others in my peer group. I try to pride myself to not be like that toward others, and when I think about why I am acting that way, it always boils down to some small petty human emotion. If I remove that emotion, then my view about the person goes from animosity and jealousy to respect and understanding. It's truly amazing. It's not easy, but if you find yourself being the personal attacker, it takes lots of self-control and reflection to remove that from your life. In my experience, most personal attacks are super small and petty, and if you propagate them, it will be a huge impediment to your career. Huge. If you are spreading ill will about others in your peer group, how can anyone trust you to lead? It's small and immature and shows that you are not ready to be a leader. You lack confidence. Don't put those shackles on yourself.

I have really good friends who are absolutely personal attackers. Jon Gordon's book, *The Energy Bus*, calls them energy vampires. Whatever you call them, you probably know the type. Having lunch, dinner, or drinks with them includes lots of gossiping, griping, and attacking various people you work with or associate. It's generally a negative experience, and if you're not careful, you can also fall into the trap of going into personal attacker mode just to connect on that person's level. It's an uncomfortable place to be. Grounding yourself in your ideals, principles, and confidence is the best way to keep yourself void of such pitfalls. Be true to yourself and the wrinkles will iron themselves out. Being humble is also key to confidence.

I'm a big fan of humility and self-deprecating humor. If you are someone who makes fun of yourself, then you don't take yourself too seriously, you have a sense of humor, and are open to listening to others. You have charisma. Many of the best leaders I have ever worked with (or for) have been very talented and very humble. In many ways, there isn't a higher "value match" of skill sets than being talented and humble. I LOVE people like that. Those that have so much ability and talent but have a fundamental understanding of the universal truth that no one is perfect. What better leader to follow than someone who gets it at that fundamental of a level?

I'll probably sound like an old man in saying this, but in today's day and age, there are a lot of people thumping their chest at any hint of success. Those of us who have to pound our chest or gesticulate about our successes, regardless of how trivial, are probably the ones with the *least* amount of confidence. The best leaders are those that know how good they are and don't need to remind everyone around them of their success or talent. I aspire to be the leader who doesn't need to pat myself on the back and can lead my team with wisdom and confidence, regardless of the situation. The dirty little secret here is that those leaders that have the skill and talent but don't flaunt it are the ones that command the most respect.

In Summary

One of the guarantees in your life as a leader will be encountering the personal attack. The personal attack will undoubtedly bring out lots of emotions in any person or leader and being able to navigate those emotions will define how well (or poorly) you handle those circumstances. With every bump in the road, there is always a wrinkle, and with personal attacks, the wrinkles get into areas of self-reflection and thoughtfulness on how to deal with those issues. Dealing with these attacks swiftly and decisively is key to your success in being able to overcome these negative and tricky situations.

LTF Action Steps:

1. Be slow to anger
2. Ignore altered states of reality
3. Deal with the attacks but don't chase them all

Chapter 7 – You

Leslie was frustrated. Leslie was a leader within Human Resources at her company and had been very successful in her career. Her current position was a big jump in responsibility from her previous roles and she was unsure in her ability to play this position at such a high level. She was also paid handsomely, which meant very high expectations for her and her teams. The problem was her team stunk.

Leslie's teams seemed to bicker and fight amongst each other, they never met project milestones, and continuously ran over budget. In all of these failures, she was able to place the blame onto one of her more junior team members, so she never really got caught up in the "bad press" but still the team struggled. Leslie spent hours pouring over her team's performance and what they needed to do better in order to perform at a higher level. Through this analysis, she was reminded of the fact that she hired many of her direct reports and that they were all-stars in their jobs prior to joining the company. She had even worked with some of them directly and saw the excellence first hand. She just couldn't put her finger on what the issue was and why the morale was so low.

To make matters worse, she had a huge <u>performance</u> coming up where she was presenting to the board of directors and had to explain a recent project <u>failure</u>. She also had the burden of having deep conflict with someone in her peer group. She simply could not partner with this <u>nemesis</u> and they were starting to take <u>personal attacks</u> on her abilities and recent failures that she would surely have to defend during the presentation to the board. She was really struggling to <u>create</u> innovative ideas and ways to dig out of these issues, and it was starting to turn into a <u>crisis</u> as several key team members had recently resigned. One sleepless night as Leslie was pacing in the bathroom, thinking about her team's problems and how they could improve, she suddenly paused, turned, and looked in the mirror and wondered…, "maybe the problem isn't them…"

++++

It's all about you. Seriously, it is *all* about you. Those people who say, "The world doesn't revolve around you" are totally wrong. The world does revolve around you but maybe not in the traditional sense of the saying. What I am referring to is your shortcomings and flaws. Those things are certainly all about you, and there is only one person who can do anything about them. *You.* This is your life and you should enjoy success in every facet of it and also have some fun along the way. But before we talk about you, let's get some perspective.

Perspective is relative to each individual. It's how you see the world, how you interpret your surroundings and the events of your life. Running for 26.2 miles for many people would seem like hell on earth and a fate worse than death. Some other people, however, view the same event and circumstances very differently. I *live* for running 26.2 miles. I have become less enchanted with running marathons now that I have kids and want to spend more time with them, but it is still a passion. It fuels me to get up early in the morning to train, spend time away from my family (whom I love more than anything on this earth), and put my body through a torture chamber of hard work, sweat, and tears. What is the difference between a person who sees running a marathon as torture and the one that lives for it? Obviously it can be a lot of things (ability, upbringing, where you live, culture, etc.), but more than anything, it is your perspective. Why do some people cherish the delicious taste and experience of consuming alcohol and others view it as a poison that leaves them feeling out of control and sick the following day. Why do some people value the relationship with their religious beliefs so satisfying and see it as a source of unlimited strength in their lives while others view religion and spirituality as an antiquated belief system based on old world ideals? It all comes down to you.

Your enjoyment of anything and how you deal with life's challenges come down to your individual wants, desires, and interests. Why is all of this important? Simply to illustrate that YOU are in control of your life and how much you enjoy it. It's up to you in determining how well you are able to navigate around the bumps of life. In this chapter, I am going to ask you to be selfish. Focusing on yourself will allow you to transform into a great leader for your employees, family, and your friends. I am also going to encourage you to look at your actions and behavior, not in the first person, but in the third. Think about your actions and behavior as if you were another person. Just like Michael Jackson famously sang, "I'm talking 'bout the man in the mirror and I'm asking him to change his ways." Self-reflection, looking at yourself as if in a mirror, is a powerful tool and will enable you to truly work on those areas where you need to improve and produce meaningful results.

There is a very good reason this chapter comes last in the book. Hopefully the material so far provided you with solid thoughts and insight to consider when you hit those fundamental challenges in your leadership journey…with the exception of this chapter. Many of the bumps we have already covered are very visible and obvious to all parties impacted. If there is a crisis going on in your life, most people would know about it. If you have a nemesis in your life, likely the other person is aware. But personal faults and shortcomings are not always readily apparent to yourself or others who may be impacted by your issues. The bottom line is most of us have a very hard time admitting our own faults and shortcomings. In order to improve yourself, there needs to be a few things in place for any book, coaching, or feedback to work. The reader has to have two things:

1.   A true want to improve yourself
2.   A realistic view of your strengths and weaknesses.

That's it. If you don't have any desire to improve yourself or think "your stuff don't stink," then there's really no point in continuing this chapter. Move to the end of the book and call it a day. But I'd argue that everyone at every phase of their life or career has room to improve upon something. Those that think contrary to that are just wrong and likely their ego or humility is getting in the way to becoming the best version of themselves. The sooner you can grasp those things, the better off you'll be. Wanting to become a better leader is a concept most can understand and desire to attain. Recognizing your strengths and weaknesses is a whole other story…

People's shortcomings in life are often times a very difficult thing to deal with or even to notice. My guess is that this is due, in large part, to the fact that we cannot see ourselves act, speak, or behave. Unless you carry around a mirror all day, what you see day in and day out is the actions and behaviors of others. It is easy for us to focus on others and not reflect inward because our primary senses (sight and hearing) are so outwardly focused that it is hard to take the focus away from that. Think about the time that you heard your voice on a voicemail or recording and how foreign it sounded. *Do I really sound like that?* I had thought my voice sounded much more professional, mature, manly, or whatever until I heard myself on a recording. We can look around and immediately see others behaviors, actions, how they speak, their appearance, and immediately see things about them that are much more difficult to see in ourselves. This is why people so easily talk or gossip about others.

Seeing our strengths and weaknesses is not easy and is the main reason why we all need coaching and advice. Because how we deal with life is such an individual and personal thing, not being able to see ourselves and our flaws makes dealing with those challenges of life very difficult...especially when the bump is us.

So how do you find out your faults? For those of you who are reading this and know immediately what your areas for improvement are, congratulations! You have reached a critical point of self-awareness. You realize this is just who you are and are committed to improving yourself to the best of your ability. You also hopefully realize that you will never be perfect, but you can be a better version of who you are today. Awesome!

For the vast majority of those of us out there who might be reading this right now and do not know your shortcomings, it's going to be okay. There are simple ways to assess your weaknesses to help you better become self-aware and work toward improvement. The way to self-identify your faults is by:

- Being Open
- Being Critical

Before we go further, you need to first strap on your thick skin. Most people *cannot* handle constructive criticism on themselves, and any and all feedback falls on deaf ears or even makes them mad, furious, or angry. While it is not productive to feel this way, it is very natural. You need to get over the fact that you are not perfect. Get over it. Only one person has been perfect. You are not a special snowflake. The reality is that the most successful business people, parents, politicians, or whomever have really acute strengths and have minimized their weaknesses. The key is that they do actually have weaknesses. Remember that success in the You category is not having *zero* faults but rather being self-aware of your faults and continually working to minimize them and grow your strengths. A perfect you is not fault free. You must be open to the fact that regardless of your level of success or stature in life you are not perfect and you never will be. So did you do it? Did you put on your thick skin? Are you ready to accept the fact that you have areas on which you can improve? If you've done that, then being critical is a walk in the park. There are several examples of very successful people who have addressed their shortcomings…

We'll start with the story of Richard Branson. He founded Virgin Records, Virgin Airlines and more generally the Virgin Group, which is made up of hundreds of companies and other ventures. Richard is known for his big ideas. He is an innovator and a maverick. He is also one of the richest people in the entire world but didn't start out that way. Richard had dyslexia and did poorly in school when he was growing up in the United Kingdom. While he struggled in school, he was able to discover at a young age that he had an uncanny knack for connecting with people. He was able to convert his scholastic struggles into a strength by building relationships and focusing on others. Allegedly on the last day of school one year, the school principal forecasted that Richard would either wind up in jail or become a millionaire. Turns out he was wrong on both fronts... Richard is not in jail and he became a *billionaire*. Richard's story is proof that even the most successful leaders have challenges and shortcomings. By being open with yourself, you can realize these areas and build a solid path forward.

Right. So now you agree that you aren't perfect, so let's find some faults. Some might say a little self-reflection and quiet time will help you identify your weaknesses. Doesn't everyone really know their faults deep down anyway? Yes, most people do know their weaknesses, but you need to take it a step farther and be *critical* of yourself. As if you were talking about someone else. No one should know you better than you. If you take the time to slow down and be very critical of yourself, it can be very rewarding. I often times discourage negativity as it can be so disruptive in your life. When trying to improve yourself, however, this is the one time negativity can help. Getting to the core of what you can improve requires you to be overcritical, and in doing so, you can start to build yourself up. I want you to be critical on both your strengths *and* weaknesses. The things you do well, what can be done better? The things you stink at, get to the core of what isn't working. Going deep and being *critical* is a hallmark of high levels of success. Tiger Woods in his heyday was known for being very critical and honest of his game. He would do a press conference after a round in a major tournament where he would shoot a fantastic score, be leading the tournament, and only talk about the one putt he missed where he should have made it. The list goes on of very successful people being critical of themselves or their teams. Our typical reaction to this seemingly masochist approach is for these leaders to lighten up and not be so critical. But perhaps it is us who should be more critical of ourselves.

So now that we've agreed we aren't perfect and that we have some specific things to address, what happens next? Should we focus on our strengths? Should we improve upon our faults and weaknesses? Should we just give up? As always, the answer lies somewhere in the middle. Being open and critical on your strengths *and* weaknesses can lead you to discover strengths you didn't even know you had. Both your strengths and weaknesses can be bumps on your leadership path if you don't take them seriously.

> Being open and critical on your strengths and weaknesses can lead you to discover strengths you didn't even know you had.

To overcome your own personal strengths and weaknesses on your leadership journey requires focus on several key areas. These focus areas include:

- Your effort level
- Ignoring your inner voice
- Trying new things
- Seeking help
- The power of opposites

Focusing on these things will help make sure your personal shortcomings don't become your downfall as a leader.

Try Your Hardest

I'm a big fan of perspective but not so much of a fan of advice. What is the difference you might ask? Advice, in my opinion, is telling someone what to do in a certain situation or circumstance. Advice assumes you know what the best course of action is for a certain person or situation…which is crazy. Perspective is telling someone how *you* dealt with a similar situation, so they can consider another point of view, but ultimately allows the person to draw their own conclusion. How someone else dealt with a personal shortcoming can allow you to potentially apply those learnings to your own situation (again, my opinion). I hate giving advice. It assumes the person doesn't know what to do. Often times people think they need advice, when in reality, they just need perspective. For people I mentor and coach, I will try to provide some perspective by telling stories on how I dealt with similar situations, but the best way to provide perspective is by asking questions. The famous Greek philosopher Socrates was *the* master at asking questions. The Socratic Method, named after Socrates, of course, is an approach for generating thought and perspective by asking lots of questions. And it works. When faced with a challenge in dealing with yourself, it is important to be reflective and ask yourself several questions to start to address these things. It's asking these questions that will help get you moving in the right direction and spurn you forward in addressing these tough situations. It will give you great perspective. One great question I like to ask people is regarding their work ethic. Does your effort level equal your talent level?

Most of the time we don't have major things wrong with us where we need to immediately stop or start doing something different. Sure we all have flaws, but most of the time they aren't fatal. In most cases, our real challenge is that we are not maximizing those things we do really well…our talents. Think back to earlier in this chapter when you thought about those things you do naturally well. Those things you enjoy doing and where you excel. Communication? Analyzing data? Leading big projects? Playing a particular sport? Running marathons? Are you utilizing those talents to their max? I can honestly say I am not. Certainly not all the time. Think about a time where you have interacted with someone either at work or in a social setting. Do you remember thinking that person is really good at what they do? Wow, they are GOOD. It's a perfect match of what they naturally do well (their talent) and the result of years of practice and honing that skill (effort). By putting lots of energy and effort into an area in which you excel, it can become an amazing combination.

A common example I use is when dining out and being the recipient of top-notch service. I was with my wife at a nice restaurant and we were celebrating our anniversary. The waiter walked over to us and their confidence and communication skills were immediately noticeable. They were in total control of every facet of the situation. They knew the menu perfectly, they spoke clearly and concisely, they wove in some humor during the discussion, and advised of food pairings with wine. The waiter articulated the specials so well, it made my mouth water. This person was not pushy and gave us time to make our decision. They answered all questions perfectly and sprinkled in a bit of charm and we never felt like anything was out of place or that we had to wait for anything. They timed the food coming out perfectly with our appetizer and entrees. It was flawlessly executed. This person was excellent at their job. It was pretty amazing actually. They clearly had charisma (talent) and had worked before in the restaurant industry, likely at this particular restaurant, for some period of time (effort). Point being is that this person brought together the full package of maximizing their talents and put forth a solid amount of effort.

Many times our talents are not maximized through our effort and this is hugely challenging for most of us out there. What is your #1 skill? How often do you use it? It's really cool when we see that combination of talent and effort packaged together like the waiter experience I just mentioned. While the waiter example is easy to grasp, there's always good visible examples of this phenomenon in the sporting world.

If you're a sports nut like me, I always think back to Michael Jordan. MJ. His Airness. He is the GOAT (Greatest of All Time) when it comes to basketball. Not only was he the most talented player each time he stepped on a basketball court, but his effort level and desire to win was fanatical. He knew in every fiber of his being and through hours and days and years of preparation that no one was going to beat him if he didn't want them to. Michael had skill and athleticism that had not been seen at the shooting guard position ever before. He was 6'6" and had quickness like a smaller guard and could jump out of the building (Air Jordan, remember?). Aside from his stellar athletic ability, his competitiveness and work ethic was also second to none. He was known for constantly challenging teammates in practice and being a tireless worker. Talk of his work habits were legendary.

The NBA players who were part of the 1992 USA Olympic basketball team tell legendary stories about Michael's fanatical drive and work ethic in the practices during the Olympic Games in 1992. The practices. Not the game. But the practices. These were some of the best players in the world, Magic Johnson, Larry Bird, David Robinson, and the list goes on and all of them were in awe. Even as his amazing athletic ability slowly started to fade later in his career, he developed his post-up game so he could score over smaller players using that infamous turn around jump shot that was almost indefensible. That combination of amazing talent and effort for Michael led to six NBA titles, five Most Valuable Player awards, 14 NBA all-star appearances, and countless scoring titles just to name a few. Not everyone can be Michael Jordan, but the reality is that you can excel in your personal and professional life by simply recognizing your talents and working to sharpen and enhance them as if they were weaknesses. Michael's career really didn't turn the corner until he started working hard in the pre-season and during the regular season. He had the raw ability, but it wasn't until the effort part kicked in that his teams started winning. He lifted weights during the pre-season and worked tirelessly on conditioning to get himself ready and healthy for the actual season and playoffs. 82 games is a long season, and even when you're Michael Jordan, talent alone is not the answer. Michael has even carried that work ethic into the front office in his current role as an NBA owner. The GOAT never sleeps...

So I'll ask it again, does your effort level equal your talent level? My guess is that you have room to improve. If you want to be the Michael Jordan of the boardroom, Michael Jordan of your home life, Michael Jordan of anything, you need to put in some work. The amount of work you put in will be directly proportional to your success in that area.

Different from Michael Jordan, there are countless others you can think of who have squandered huge amounts of talent during their lifetime. This is why the question of work ethic and overcoming your imperfections is so critical. Talent wasted is such a pity, so you should constantly evaluate your work ethic and make sure you aren't taking shortcuts. What if Michael decided to take the easy way out and not put in all the work? Maybe he would have not even made it to the NBA or his college team. What if you aren't putting in the work and you could have a much higher ceiling then what you are achieving today. Put in the work and you will overcome your flaws and maximize your strengths. The good news is the choice is up to you.

Try Something New?
Do you talk about those things where you struggle? Your weaknesses? I have to be honest here, I am really bad at this. I'm not sure if it's

pride or wanting to conceal those things that I struggle with, but I do not talk about those things…at all. If you've ever been in a professional interview at some point in your career, someone will ask you, "What is your greatest strength and what is your greatest weakness?" It's such a bologna question! Here is my answer every time someone asks me that question, "I work too hard when I should let up sometimes and get balance in my life." What an awful, bogus answer that is. Lame. Other bogus answers include, "I am too detail-oriented," "I take my work too seriously," "I'm a perfectionist." All of those are strengths hidden in a disguise of weakness.

We simply do not own our weaknesses, which is essentially lying about who we really are. Think about it. Why are we so afraid to expose ourselves for who we really are? Wouldn't our potential employer value the fact that we are brutally honest about ourselves and what we bring to the table? The answer is yes, they would, but we tell ourselves that the prospective employer wouldn't want to hire someone who can sometimes get stressed out and overwhelmed when the work starts to pile up. Or hire a person that holds things in and sometimes could do a better job of communicating things more broadly (all of those last ones are me by the way). Your employer is going to find out about your strengths and weaknesses at some point, so why draw that out and delay the inevitable?

I talked a lot about confidence in this book because it is so key to overcome all these challenges you will face in your life and career. Being strong or confident in the face of challenges helps you overcome just about everything. A really good question to ask yourself is why aren't you confident in certain areas? Is it because you just don't have the skill? Is it because you just don't like doing that certain thing (hey, I hate working with spreadsheets, so I really don't think I am good at it!)? Or is it because you've never really tried something *new* to improve yourself? If it's the latter, then you have a real opportunity to find out something about yourself. If you've never put forth any effort in trying to do something new, how can you really know if you are good at it? You cannot. The reason trying something new is critical to overcoming your faults is because we live in an ever-changing

> ...trying something new is critical to overcoming your faults is because we live in an ever-changing world

world. If your strength is public speaking, just think how much that has changed with the advent of YouTube, Ted Talks, and social media. If you never try something new, suddenly that strength of yours is no longer relevant and the innovators have passed you by. Constant personal growth is key to your success as a leader and it can happen at any age in life. Ever hear of Taikichiro Mori?

Taikichiro Mori, at one point, was the richest man in the world and was worth $13 billion or two times the net worth of Bill Gates at his peak. Taikichiro spent the first 55 years of his life in obscurity working as an economics professor in Japan and not really having any interest in real estate, other than the fact that his father owned two buildings in addition to being a humble rice farmer. Upon his father's death, Taikichiro inherited the meek family business (few buildings in downtown Japan) and grew it into approximately 83 high rise buildings in downtown Tokyo, which is considered some of the most expensive real estate in the world. He built a juggernaut empire out of almost nothing simply by trying something new!

I do not know Mr. Mori personally, but assume that through his economics studies, he had some business acumen but had not made his living on real estate development or entrepreneurial endeavors when he took over the family business at age 55. He was a textbook guy who had a ton of book smarts and intellect. Clearly he had some amazing skills and talents that lay dormant within him for years. Prior to his crazy success, I wonder if someone might have said that Taikichiro had room to improve on applying his textbook knowledge in the "real world." Maybe you have a hidden talent that is an untapped treasure within you but simply haven't given it a chance to flourish. Think about that the next time you are resisting to try something new. Maybe a little application and effort around those weaknesses can make you into the next Taikichiro Mori.

Who Needs Self-Preservation?

Why does all of this matter anyway? So what? Who cares if I am not great at everything and don't put 100% effort into my strengths or my weaknesses? I have kids, a spouse, a job, and not much time for anything else. Why should I work on these things? Well, the reality is that those who are losing in life simply don't put forth effort into anything. They don't put a priority on trying to improve their shortcomings, much less trying to improve the things they already do well. If you

> If you want to be like everyone else, then you should continue to do what you've been doing as you will continue to get the same results

want to be like everyone else, then you should continue to do what you've been doing as you will continue to get the same results. The definition of insanity seems to apply here, "continuing to do the same thing over and over again and expecting different results."

Even more fundamental than negotiating the time management piece of this is something deeper down inside of every human. Each of us has a built-in mechanism around self-preservation. If you have ever run a marathon or done something very physically challenging, you know this voice well. It's the voice inside your head that shouts at you to stop. It's this voice that says *running 20 miles is plenty. Why go the extra 6.2 miles? Twenty miles is an amazing accomplishment. You can stop right here, no one would blame you. Running that far is HARD. Not many people can run a marathon, so you should stop right now! Don't push your limits. You're safe right here!* I'm sure you have heard the voice of self-preservation many times before in a variety of settings. That voice is very conservative and sounds off when you need it the least. This is also the same voice that tells you *not* to improve upon your weaknesses. This voice is not a bad thing, in fact, it is lifesaving in some situations, but it is also a serious barrier to pushing beyond our comfort zone and limitations. The self-preservation voice sounds off, not only on physical endeavors, but also in professional and social situations as well. Anytime when you need to preserve yourself, be it physical, emotional, or whatever, this voice is hard wired to sound off and protect the wholeness of you. It's actually kind of amazing to think about. It's probably a great example of natural selection. Back a long time ago, I'm sure our caveman ancestors needed this voice to keep them alive. Those cavemen who had this voice in their head may not have pushed their physical limits and been able to save energy or food and make it through a drought or slow hunting spell. Similarly, this same voice may have kept the caveman right in the middle of the social hierarchy and kept them safe from power struggles or from being ostracized from the pack. It might have also kept them safe from predators of the time by being a little tentative when leaving the cave. Some people have a very strong voice of self-preservation and it is a fascinating thing to consider. Always remember that the process of natural selection and your parents gave you this voice and that ignoring it can at times be the best thing you can do. This voice wants to keep you safe and no leader will ever excel by always playing it safe. You have to sometimes ignore the voice and stretch your comfort zone. If you want a good example of someone who is an expert at ignoring that inner voice of self-preservation to improve themselves and maximize their results, look no further than Scott Jurek.

Scott is a legend in the sport of ultra-marathon running. If you thought running a plain old 26.2-mile marathon was nuts, then you're going to think Scott is one step away from the looney bin. Scott has won and set records in races over 100 miles long with some of those races going up to 135+ miles! There was one race in particular that was chronicled in the amazing book "Born to Run" where Scott was running the Badwater Ultramarathon. The Badwater Ultramarathon is a 135-mile race that starts below sea level and runs you up to an elevation of 8,000+ feet. If that wasn't bad enough, you also run through Death Valley in California where temperatures can exceed 120-degrees Fahrenheit. At some point, I hope to understand why someone would want to run this race and maybe even meet the sadistic person who came up with the idea in the first place. Regardless, Scott Jurek is a legend in these types of races.

On one particular race in 2005, Scott was more than halfway into the event and his body was shutting down from the excessive heat and exhaustion. He was stopped on the side of the road with his crew contemplating pulling out of the race as he was fighting against the crushing conditions of Death Valley, and that voice inside his head was screaming at him to STOP. Very clearly his body was also saying STOP with several physical ailments popping up. His main competitor was getting a lead on him and his body was shutting down. Instead of listening to that voice of doubt, he pulled himself up off the ground, blasted the remaining portion of the course, winning the race and setting a course record all the while beating his main competitor. Wow. Had he listened to that voice, where would he be now? Maybe still on the side of the road! Who knows for sure, but he didn't listen and something truly amazing happened. While we may not need to go to that extreme level in our own lives, what if we ignored that voice every now and then? It just might yield amazing results.

When something goes wrong in our life, whether it be personal or professional, one of the first things we do as humans is look to assign blame to someone else. Think about the last time something went haywire where you were directly involved in some manner. Whether you were right in the middle of it or on the periphery, you assigned the blame elsewhere. *They* should have communicated better. *He* didn't dig into the details. *She* wasn't able to close the deal effectively. This deflection is the easy way out and it is that same voice of self-preservation we all have that keeps us safe. It keeps us whole. It's happens easily because it's what comes natural, it's how we are wired. All of this is deflecting whatever the issue is onto someone else so that we can maintain our oneness. The reality is that true growth comes out of pain. Pushing that boundary in physical training is what allows athletes and weekend warriors alike to improve. Breaking away from keeping yourself in tact is what true leaders do. What if Scott Jurek listened to that inner voice and tried to preserve himself? True leaders do not always listen to the voice of self-preservation. True leaders think first about how they can own the situation and make it better. *I* didn't communicate effectively. *I* should have helped more on the details. *I* wasn't a good partner to help close the deal. Owning up to your shortcomings, both inwardly and outwardly, can pay major dividends. Having your co-workers or family members hear the area or situation where you could have done better lets them know you are not perfect and are accessible. This person does not sit in an ivory tower of perfectness that is not accessible by anyone else. This person is in the trenches just like me. Inwardly accepting fault and acknowledging your flaws is a huge step toward admitting you're not perfect and are committed to improving yourself. Everyone points toward someone else when something goes wrong. So what? Why don't you change that dynamic and become a true leader by owning your flaws and ignoring the voice of self-preservation. Everyone, including yourself, will be better off for it.

Help Yourself...

In many situations there is a wrinkle in your plan. Sometimes there is an obstacle that, despite your wants and needs, there is just an exception to the rule. The insights and experiences noted above apply to most folks and can help provide perspective on how to treat certain circumstances related to your own personal shortcomings. But there are always exceptions to the rules. I consider myself a fairly decent coach and mentor. It is something I have a lot of passion around and take pride in how I am able to help other people. But despite my passion, insight, and real-world experiences, it is very difficult to apply those skills to one person in particular. Myself.

As noted previously, it is hard to see yourself objectively, especially when talking about your faults. It is one of our hard-wired defense mechanisms and can be an impediment to truly dissecting our faults and making strides in resolving them. While I firmly believe that with even minimal investment in self-reflection and hard work, anyone can grow and develop themselves, there can still be gaps that need a different approach. Sometimes even the best insight and self-reflection cannot fully address a shortcoming that has grown and developed over the course of your lifetime. You may not even be aware that something is an issue or character fault until you really invest some time with a professional coach, mentor, or really good therapist. You should not go it alone.

For some people, there is a stigma with seeking the help from these types of professionals and this is a stereotype we must tear down. I, too, was someone who did not believe in seeking professional help on some of my shortcomings until I tried it one time, and now I am a firm believer. Being able to discuss your own challenges with a skilled professional is incredibly therapeutic. The act of being vulnerable to someone and not having that person judge you but rather listen and try to help is extremely uplifting. Many people see the inability to independently solve your own problems as a weakness or something necessary only for a crazy person. I would argue that those *not* seeking help with their issues from a skilled professional or mentor are the ones who are going about this all the wrong way. Having a coach, therapist, mentor, psychologist, or whatever in your life can be an incredible asset and can help you address those things you simply cannot remedy on your own.

All of the best leaders have some form of a coach or mentor. It's key to their success. Many top executives utilize coaches and mentors to ensure they are at the top of their game. If some of the smartest and best leaders in the professional community are using these resources, why shouldn't you? If you haven't used one of these resources, then doing so will open you up in a way you are not able to do on your own. The act of talking to a professional will help get to the root of those issues you cannot resolve on your own. Doing so will result in personal growth that otherwise would not be possible on your own.

Another wrinkle in dealing with your own personal shortcomings is success. What does that mean, you might ask? Well, if you are one of those lucky people who is successful in both your personal life and professional career, then many might wonder why you should change anything at all? Even if you're not wildly successful but are one of those people who is content in your life, then why would you move things around? Shake things up? Why improve on your shortcomings or faults if they clearly are not slowing you down on your path in life. I am one of those people who firmly believes that if it ain't broke, then don't fix it. You really should never mess with happiness (or success for that matter) but the flaw in that thinking is that it is very inwardly focused and there is *always* something to improve upon. Even if you are successful or happy, it doesn't mean that there isn't something you can improve upon. This is where getting help from a mentor or advisor can pay huge dividends. They can help you see things you cannot and bring a different perspective to most situations.

But still, give me a good reason to look for areas of improvement when you are

> The minute you stop improving, learning, and growing is the same minute you start to erode

already happy and successful? It's hard, but you gotta do it and here's why. The minute you stop improving, learning, and growing is the same minute you start to erode. It's somewhat cliché but it's very true. It's called ego. Those of you out there thinking that you are successful and do not need to improve may have a bit of an ego problem…you might be in denial. The history books are littered with examples of folks that were at the top of their game, got complacent, and ended up having a huge fall from grace. Look no further than William Orton. Who is William Orton, you may ask? That is my point exactly.

William Orton was the one-time president of Western Union, and his overconfidence led to one of the larger "misses" in corporate history. Western Union was the dominant player in the telegraph industry in the 19th century, and their telegrams were a part of pop culture appearing in movies, magazines, and everything in between. Western Union was formed from multiple different telegraph companies and eventually helped to make a unified transcontinental telegraph system in the 1850's (pretty cool science fiction type stuff back then). Ezra Cornell, the famous New York businessman, had his fingerprints all over the merger that made Western Union the powerhouse that it was back in the 1860 timeframe. The merger that was facilitated by Cornell ultimately set the company up to be one of the first monopolies in U.S. history and also earned it a spot on the Dow Jones Transportation Average of the New York Stock Exchange. Now as you might guess, in the mid 1870's, Western Union was at the top of the competitive market when it came to the telegraph industry, but there was a new guy in town and his name was the telephone. Alexander Graham Bell and many other scientists were in an arms race trying to develop the original version of the telephone. It was a far less scientific version than what we have today but a tool that allowed tones and utterances to be transmitted over a wire. Again, science fiction for the day. In addition to Bell, there were several other scientists trying to get the golden patent that locked them in as the "creator" of the modern day telephone, allowing them to corner the market and make it a viable product. Through lots of trials, tribulations, and of course, some drama, Bell was the one that ultimately got the patent (fantastic reading if you are ever interested in checking out the backstory). Almost equally as smart as the creation itself, Bell and his financial backers knew they were sitting on a potential goldmine. Bell and his team offered the patent to Western Union and then President William Orton for $100,000 (as the story goes). When offered the patent, Orton allegedly scoffed at the idea and supposedly called this new invention simply a "toy." I would assume that Orton probably didn't think the almighty Western Union needed something like that when they were already on top of the world as it related to the telegraph industry. He was cocky. He may have also guessed this telephone thing was science fiction and not applicable for the masses. After all, Western Union was in newspapers, books, and magazines; why should they spend a lot of money on some new-fangled invention to improve themselves when they were already "great" and at the peak of their success. If anyone out there has ever climbed a mountain, you know what happens once you hit the peak…you then start the descent. Well, as you can probably guess, the telephone indeed took off and the versions that exist today continue to innovate the ways in which we interact, spend our time, communicate, invest money, play games, and everything in between. Alexander Graham Bell is forever etched in the history books as the creator of the telephone, and no one really even remembers William Orton. To his credit, two years after the original offer by Bell and his investors, Orton supposedly quipped that he would pay millions for the rights to the invention if he had the chance to do it all over again.

For those of you out there that are successful in your life or career, let the story of William Orton be a call to action to you. Regardless of your current level of success, there is always room for improvement, advancement, and innovation in your life and getting help from an outsider can help you realize this in a positive way. Speaking from personal experience, I was struggling with stress, depression, and anxiety in several facets of my life. It wasn't until I found a mentor to help me unpack these complications that I was able to break through these challenges and focus on the things that really mattered in my life. My family, my faith, and my friends. If you're not moving forward and growing, then you are simply moving backwards, and MOST of us cannot move forward without some help.

Opposites Attract (Success)

The people in life who embrace their shortcomings are the most successful. There isn't some fancy study or survey I have to substantiate this, but every boss or leader I have ever worked for, that is good at what they do, has this innate quality of being "open." They aren't afraid to let others into their world, and at the same time, are not afraid of criticism (constructive or not). Embrace your weaknesses, but most importantly, embrace your strengths. Improving upon your weaknesses is critical to success but even better than that is something far less monumental. I've heard Hunter S. Thompson and Woody Allen being credited with this quote, but whoever said it first (probably somebody else!) got it right. "Half of life is just showing up."

It truly amazes me as I interact with others and see and experience how people operate and observe their styles that this quote seems to be more and more accurate. Just show up, and in many cases, you are considered to be performing above your peers despite whatever shortcomings you may possess. More broadly than simply showing up, do the things that are expected of you. Show up on time, be professional, and don't be high maintenance. Those people that struggle professionally are the ones that always have some clutter going on around them. They are always late. They complain. They aren't professional. And probably more than anything, these people don't care about their work. Manager and leaders have enough to deal with in their normal job, and having to deal with their team's clutter is not a good use of anyone's time.

If you care about your work and put forth effort on improving those things you do well, you will be successful in life. If you work on the things you naturally do well and also those things you do not… magic can happen and your success and future can be limitless. Especially if you show up.

Many of the best leaders will take it one step further and hire people around them who complement their weaknesses. Beyond just showing up, they round out their skills with people *different* from them. If you're weak at paying attention to the details, then you better have a second-in-command who is a details wizard. If your weakness is communication, have someone who excels at communicating to the people in your organization or line of business and have them assist you in delivering key messages. I personally hire people who are very different from me and am a huge believer in diversity. Well-rounded teams normally can cover all aspects of any business issue, project, or crisis. Many organizations are focused on having a clear and concise corporate culture based on whatever value system they deem the most relevant and important. Often times the team involved in the hiring process can misinterpret this aspect of corporate culture by hiring folks that are exactly the same as them. We often times hire "people like us" because we think and act alike and do so in the name of corporate culture. My view is that culture is agnostic to skills and the way people think and process information. You can still value customer service and make that a very high priority corporate goal but be a stickler for details. Just like you can have the same customer service focus, hate details, but be a whiz at communicating and being creative.

Or strategic thinking. Or very technical. Or very numbers focused. Or a great listener. Just imagine a team with that variety of skills, but each person has a singular agreement that customer service is key to success. That diverse group could bring a lot to the table. Be confident in hiring people and associating with others that are different than you, especially those that complement your own shortcomings. Many successful leaders have the yen to their yang. The black to their white. The old school to their modern approach. The gentle to their rough. You get the point. One such iconic leader was very aware of her shortcomings and her addressing of these issues made a huge difference in her lifetime of success. Ever heard of Coco Chanel?

Coco Chanel was the famous Matriarch and fashion designer that created the now world-famous women's perfume Chanel No. 5. Coco was a design icon herself and her fragrance was known around the world. She influenced a new age of women's fashion coming out of post World War I and is listed as one of Time Magazine's most influential people of the 20th Century. Early in her professional career, she decided to partner with French businessman Pierre Wertheimer. What Coco had in design, creativity, and fashion, she lacked in marketing know-how and business acumen. She was, however, smart enough to realize her shortcomings and partner with Mr. Wertheimer who was a marketing whiz and astute business man in France. Pierre and his brother Paul were directors of the cosmetics house Bourgeois, and through their partnership with Coco, they provided a mechanism for her to finance, market, and promote her fragrance and fashion products (mostly Chanel No. 5). While the deal they struck initially was not very fair and equitable for Coco (it's a pretty amazing story filled with controversy and drama and worth a read), it ultimately made her a very wealthy woman and serves as a great example of how finding a complement to your known weakness can have a profound effect on your success. Would Coco have been such a massive success without the help Mr. Wertheimer? We'll never know, but what we do know is that her partnership helped catapult her into worldwide fame and fortune. What if you have that level of capability deep within you and all it needs is a complimentary skillset or person to take you to the next level? Kind of makes you think, huh?

What happens if you're not the boss and are not in a position to hire folks that compliment your skill set? Find a co-worker or acquaintance whom you trust. It's best to do this with a person where you don't have a strong relationship or past history that could cloud the nature of advice or guidance they could provide. If you have a trusted person who complements your skill set nicely, they would be honored if you asked for their help. Most of the time if you ask in a complimentary manner, people are flattered and very willing to help you out. The most important thing is to reciprocate the favor in some way. I always would ask someone I trust to proofread emails or important presentations before I would send them out or present. Often times asking folks more junior to me to provide feedback or insight on something makes them feel important and provides a gentle boost to their ego. People are truly willing to help if there is something in it for them. Find out for the particular trusted advisor if it is ego driven or fulfilling a simple need, but whatever the case, find a way to have them help you.

It might be a little harder to hire in new family members to complement your shortcomings. What I find is that in most cases the old adage of opposites attract is right on in most relationships. My wife and I are very different people in how we think and process information. In most ways, she is very much the opposite of me. It's kind of hilarious, actually how different we are in most facets of our life. But with our disparity, we bring a lot to our family nucleus. Between the two of us, we bring a wide array of thoughts and skills to the table for about any situation. Whether it be disciplining our kids, planning a vacation, purchasing a vehicle, or whatever, we bring a diverse perspective to that experience. The key is being partners in all these things. You can't just say that one partner in the relationship is good at the details, so they alone will do the budget (or whatever the case might be). In order to be effective, it has to be a partnership between the two people.

When the partnership isn't there, the strength of the two diverse perspectives is lost. Whether at work or at home, always try to complement your shortcomings by partnering with your spouse or by hiring the folks that best complement your weaknesses. All of these little secrets can really help you chip away and improve your weaknesses and help you realize your full potential. Take them seriously and look for ways to incorporate them into your life!

In Summary

Managing your own personal shortcomings is hugely critical to your success. In my opinion, it is the number one thing that can hold you back from being the best leader you can be. While I believe that half of being successful in life is just simply showing up, it's exciting to think that enhancing your strengths and building upon your weaknesses will lead you to even further success at work or at home. Owning your shortcomings is something that must be done but is never easy. It's even more difficult to look at your own issues objectively and recognize things in which you can improve however doing this is a necessary and major step in identifying and overcoming your weaknesses. All things being equal, wanting to change is the most important thing in being able to overcome the bump in life related to your shortcomings.

LTF Action Plan

1. Maximize your efforts
2. Ignore the voice that says quit and do more
3. Try one new thing a week
4. Get help from someone on something

In conclusion...Live the Fourth

So what does it all mean? So, you're saying in my journey as a leader, I'll encounter some challenges? Perhaps have a nemesis. Have to deal with a crisis. Have to ace my performances. Create something bigger than myself. Deal with failures and personal attacks on my character. Wrestle with my own shortcomings. That is a lot to take on in any one lifetime, much less having to also deal with running a successful business, division, team, or family. I'd like to think that buried within the pages of this book are some great insights, ways to deal with the challenges that come up every day, and even a couple tips to help you successfully manage these bumps along the road. The reality is that it's easy to read this book or the thousands of other leadership books and get excited and want to enact change in your life and become a better leader. I love these types of books as they are energizing and get you excited to be the best leader you can be and overcome the struggles in your life. But just like the intensity of your love for something new starts to change over time, your application of the principles in this book will also start to fade over time (even despite the top-notch skills of the author!). Despite the wisdom and insight of the pages above, it is hard to continually improve and be diligent about your own personal growth as a leader. And that is where *living the fourth comes* in...

What is living the fourth? Does it have to do with the Fourth of July? Nope. The four principles of leadership? Nah. Fourth Amendment? No, sir. Fourth Estate? C'mon. Fantastic Four? Stop it. Living the fourth (LTF) has to do with something that is a little deeper than some of the items noted above. It cuts to the heart of the matter and is the real reason why any of the above challenges in your leadership journey can be overcome.

When I was in high school, an all-boys Catholic high school, each senior class had to go on a retreat. The retreat was broken up by students who were in the same classes (generally) and was intended to be three days of spiritual reflection and exploration spent in a quiet and rural setting. The goal for these three days was to get closer to God and become more in touch with your spiritual side as you move toward adulthood and out into the real world outside of high school. For three days, you immersed yourself in this environment where there wasn't much else to do other than reflect and think about these things. It was very easy to get excited and energized in this safe cocoon where there were no other distractions and your singular focus was on this one thing. I remember being so pumped up and euphoric in this setting and wishing this good feeling would go on forever. But it can't go on forever, and at some point, you have to leave this warm cocoon and go home to face reality. It was on the *fourth* day of the retreat that you left this beautiful setting and began to assimilate back into the real world where there are distractions and challenges to confront you at every turn (even for a high school punk like me). At the conclusion of the retreat, there was a ceremony to close out the event and the theme of that ceremony was *live the fourth*. In the retreat, for three days, you got to talk and act in a certain way and everyone around you was on the same page. But at the end of the three days, you have to leave all the talk, all the support, all the camaraderie, and all the goodwill behind. You had to put all the talk into practice and actually live what you had been discussing in this vacuum over the prior three days. You have to *live the fourth* day on your own.

Just like in my senior year retreat, I hope that this book has a profound effect on you. I hope it inspires you, challenges you, makes you look at things a little differently, gives you some insight, and gets you fired up to take on those challenges that we all face as leaders every day. But also like my senior retreat, you will eventually read all the pages of the book and will have gathered those insights relevant to yourself. Any wisdom. Any knowledge. Any lessons. All of this content will be captured while reading the book, but at the conclusion, you will have to put down the book and figure out how to overcome these daily challenges. *You* will have to live the fourth day (and beyond) according to your own rules and circumstances. You'll have to take what you learned in this book and apply it to your life outside of the safe environment that is your brain. You have to take action.

...don't just read the words in this book, feel inspired, and then revert back to your old ways. Take action. Change yourself.

So, in conclusion, don't just read the words in this book, feel inspired, and then revert back to your old ways. Take action. Change yourself. Listen to the secrets in this book. Take the examples I share and learn from them. Learn from my mistakes. Don't be afraid to make your own mistakes. These challenges will happen in your life and I want you to successfully overcome them. You can do that by being open to listen and learn from the words in this book and those of other experienced leaders around you.

Be open.

Act.

That is all. Good luck on your leadership journey. I know you can overcome all of these challenges with the right attitude and mindset. Now, go and live the *fourth*...

CPSIA information can be obtained
at www.ICGtesting.com
Printed in the USA
LVHW081257201219
641190LV00007BA/33/P